NEW HAVEN CHEF'S TABLE

restaurants

recipes &

local food connections

LINDA GIUCA and **NANCY FREEBORN**
foreword **FAITH MIDDLETON**
photographs **AMY ETRA**

LYONS PRESS
Guilford, Connecticut

An imprint of Globe Pequot Press

Lyons Press is an imprint of Globe Pequot Press.

Project Manager, Text Design and Layout: Nancy Freeborn
Project Editor: David Legere
Photography © Amy Etra
Photography on page vi © Sharon Vine, page 133 (outside, right) © Valerie Bannister.

Library of Congress Cataloging-in-Publication Data

Giuca, Linda.
  New Haven chef's table : restaurants, recipes, and local food connections / Connecticut Mental Health Center Foundation ; foreword by Faith Middleton ; text by Linda Giuca ; stories by Jan Ellen Spiegel ... [et al.] ; photographs by Amy Etra ; compiled by Nancy Freeborn.
    p. cm.
  Includes index.
  ISBN 978-0-7627-5879-1
  1. Restaurants—Connecticut—New Haven—Guidebooks. 2. Cookery—Connecticut—New Haven. 3. New Haven (Conn.)—Social life and customs. I. Title.
  TX907.3.C82.N49 2010
  647.95746'8—dc22

2010016851

Printed in China
10 9 8 7 6 5 4 3 2 1

Tell me what you eat, I'll tell you who you are.

JEAN ANTHELME BRILLAT-SAVARIN

contents

foreword

It would be foolish of me to say which city or town in Connecticut has the best food, since that would put an end to my never-ending and joyous research. And yet I can tell you that I would not start a bar brawl if someone on the stool next to mine said New Haven is the center of great food in our state.

New Haven's restaurant scene—and it is a scene—ranges from small dives, each with a single, must-have dish, to signature spots with a dizzying array of terrific choices.

There are theories about why New Haven's many restaurants are so good. Did it begin when the Shubert was a real Broadway try-out house, bringing audiences and actors with appetites for first-rate food? Or does it connect to our immigrant populations, especially the Italians from Amalfi who settled here? The truth is that no one knows for sure, and so I like to say it is some unknowable alchemy of population, ethnicity, universities, small business acumen, and luck that accounts for our culinary star status.

After thirty years of hosting *The Faith Middleton Show* on WNPR from a studio on the edge of downtown New Haven, nothing thrills me and producers Lori Mack and Cameron Henning more than prowling the city in search of the next great dish. We are often amazed that we can eat gloriously and around the world here without crossing the city border.

Please know that the celebration of New Haven restaurants you find in these pages will make you as hungry as they have made me, and that you have my thanks for supporting the Connecticut Mental Health Center, which serves more than 7,000 New Haven clients each year.

Faith Middleton
The Food Schmooze, WNPR
90.5 FM and WNPR.org

introduction

We are what we eat . . . or so the saying goes. Only now with more attention to local and sustainably grown food, microclimates, and distinctive regional cuisines, what we are when we eat is not just healthier, happier, and wiser, but more deeply connected to our communities and the source of our sustenance. As we get to know who's growing our Swiss chard and peaches, raising our chickens and goats, fishing for our striped bass and lobsters, and laying our tables with delectable feasts, we can taste greater New Haven—in all its variety—the way a connoisseur tastes the earthy terroir of a certain grape in a sip of wine.

The Connecticut Mental Health Center Foundation is pleased to bring you this wonderful new cookbook featuring recipes from New Haven's finest chefs and other stories about how food is transforming and being transformed in New Haven. At the CMHC Foundation, we believe that access to wholesome fresh food that tastes delicious and is well prepared is crucial to the health and well-being of everyone. Every day scientists and philosophers, farmers and chefs, and the like tell us that good food both nourishes and nurtures us, feeding our bodies, minds, and spirits.

The best chefs have an uncanny knack—even gift—for combining to great effect things that wouldn't ordinarily go together. In that spirit, the CMHC Foundation is dedicated to forging new and extraordinary partnerships where people work together

to make a difference in individual and community health. We are pleased to let you know that proceeds from your purchase of this cookbook will benefit the CMHC Foundation and go directly to help people with serious mental illnesses live healthy and meaningful lives in the community. Because of your purchase, we will be able to continue to give more than seven thousand people in mental health and addiction recovery financial assistance for food, clothing, and other emergency needs; we will create innovative supportive projects in

partnership with greater New Haven service agencies to improve the lives of the people we serve; and we will educate citizens about mental health and addiction issues and vital resources that are available in the community.

We are grateful to the chefs, restaurateurs, farmers, purveyors, teachers, and others without whose hospitality and participation this book would not exist. We also thank the authors Linda Giuca, Jan Ellen Spiegel, Todd Lyon, Valerie Bannister, and Anastatia Curley, and photographer Amy Etra for bringing the varieties of New Haven food experiences so vividly to life in words and pictures. We are grateful to Mike Hotchkiss who floated the initial idea for a cookbook and to Susan Woodall, Judy Nugent, and Bettyann Kevles who generously contributed their time, expertise and insight to move this book from the ficker of an idea to a work in progress. Thanks also to Michael Morand who helped us secure essential start-up funds from the Yale Office of New Haven and State Affairs. Our deepest gratitude goes to Nancy Freeborn, who, like a chef de cuisine, combined her passion for food with her exquisite creative design to bring this book from our table to yours.

My wife and I have a young son who likes to tease us when we ask him about something he's just eaten at mealtime. "I don't like it," he smiles mischievously. "I love it!" I trust you will love these recipes and glimpses of New Haven's vibrant and interconnected food community.

To your health and well-being and with our heartfelt thanks,

Kyle Pedersen, Director
The Connecticut Mental Health Center Foundation
New Haven, Connecticut

116 crown

executive chef | Michael Denisiewicz

Behind the bar, John Ginnetti is a purist. "A martini is gin, vermouth, and a twist," says John, who, with his wife, Danielle, opened the hip, slick gathering place in 2007. "That's where I dig in my heels to preserve the sanctity" of the drink, he says.

John's commitment to fresh ingredients, proper techniques, and consistency as he describes an expertly-made drink as a "celebration of each ingredient" applies equally to the eclectic, Mediterranean-inspired menu.

Working with seasonal foods leads to a menu that changes quarterly, and frequently more often as new foods come to market. The couple and their kitchen and bar staffs work together to create a balance between the food and drink. After all, John points out, "An apéritif opens the appetite and readies the palate for the food to follow."

116 Crown is first and foremost a restaurant, but the Ginnettis designed the space with both cocktails and food in mind. "There are enough seats so people come in for cocktails and a bite to eat, or nothing to eat at all, or for dinner with a cocktail, or wine with dinner and a digestif," John says.

116 Crown St. | 203.777.3116
116crown.com

Plum Frost

The bar at 116 Crown, well known for its innovative mixings, goes all out with this delicious combination of specialty liquors. Sweet Japanese plum wine, crystal-clear Vermont White vodka, French ginger liqueur Domaine de Canton, Luxardo Triplum triple sec, and finally, a hint of cinnamon rimming the glass, combine to further indulge your taste buds. Perfection!

Cinnamon

2 ounces plum wine

1 ounce Vermont White vodka

½ ounce Domaine de Canton

½ ounce Luxardo Triplum triple sec

Edible flower for garnish

1. Chill a martini glass in the freezer.

2. Rim the edge of the martini glass with cinnamon (the frost will make the cinnamon stick).

3. In a chilled metal mixing cup, combine the four liquors and stir until ice appears on cup.

4. Double-strain liquor into the glass and garnish with an edible flower.

Matthew McGourty

Owner Patrick Mansfield
and Shane Carty

anna liffey's & the playwright

executive chefs | Shane Carty & Matthew McGourty

Step through the doors of Anna Liffey's or the Playwright, and be prepared to experience the rustic, noisy pubs of the Emerald Isle. Televised soccer matches, imported brews, music, and bartenders and chefs with Irish brogues are on tap.

On the menus are traditional Irish dishes such as shepherd's pie, fish and chips, and Guinness stew. "It's nice pub food, warm food," says Matthew McGourty, a manager and bartender at The Playwright. In addition to lunch and dinner fare at Anna Liffey's, a hearty Irish breakfast awaits die-hard soccer fans who spend Saturday mornings watching matches on the television.

Anna Liffey's attracts a diverse crowd that beckons even head chef Shane Carty in his off-duty hours. "When I'm not working I come down here as well. Everyone seems to know everyone. It's pretty fun here."

Anna Liffey's
17 Whitney Ave. | 203.773.1776
annaliffeys.com

The Playwright
1232 Whitney Ave., Hamden | 203.287.2401
playwrightirishpub.com

Shepherd's Pie

[Anna Liffey's]

Shane Carty, head chef at Anna Liffey's, says his shepherd's pie is one of the most popular dishes on the menu and one of the easiest items to make at home.

For the mashed potatoes:

1 pound potatoes, peeled and chopped

Salt and freshly ground black pepper

1½ cups milk

2 tablespoons butter

For the filling:

1 pound ground beef (80 percent lean/ 20 percent fat)

1 large onion, finely chopped

2 small carrots, diced

½ cup ketchup

1½ cups fresh peas, cooked

1½ cups beef gravy

Salt and freshly ground black pepper

¼ cup grated cheddar cheese

1. Preheat the broiler. Boil potatoes in salted water until soft when pierced with a knife.

2. While potatoes are cooking, brown ground meat in a frying pan over medium-high heat. When meat is cooked, drain excess oil and remove from pan. Set aside.

3. In the same pan, saute the onion and carrots over medium-high heat until soft. Stir in cooked ground beef, ketchup, peas, and gravy. Season with salt and pepper. Bring mixture to a boil and then remove from heat.

4. When potatoes are cooked, drain off the water. Add milk and butter and mash together until smooth. Season with salt and pepper.

5. Pour the hot beef mixture into a baking dish, cover with hot mashed potatoes (we use a pastry bag with a large star tip), and sprinkle with cheddar cheese.

6. Broil for 3 to 4 minutes or until cheese is melted.

> I grew up with my mother cooking these dishes as a lad, so the fun memories I get when I make them for my customers is a real joy.
>
> —SHANE CARTY, HEAD CHEF AT ANNA LIFFEY'S

Guinness Stew

[The Playwright]

When the Irish people began immigrating to the United States, fleeing from the ravages of starvation caused by the potato famine, they naturally brought along their wonderful hearty food traditions. Our famous Guinness stew evolved and adapted to include the local offerings. Sheep were not as plentiful in America, so other types of meat, such as beef, were often substituted.

1. Heat olive oil in large, heavy pot over medium-high heat. Add beef, and sauté until brown on all sides, about 5 minutes.

2. Add garlic, and sauté for 1 minute.

3. Add demi-glace, Worcestershire sauce, Guinness, and bay leaves. Stir to combine, and bring mixture to a boil.

4. Reduce to medium-low heat, cover, and simmer for 1 hour, stirring occasionally.

5. While the meat and demi-glace are simmering, melt butter in another large pot over medium heat. Add potatoes, onion, and carrots. Sauté until golden, about 20 minutes. Set aside.

6. When beef mixture is done simmering, add vegetables. Simmer uncovered until vegetables and beef are very tender, about 40 minutes. Discard bay leaves. Tilt pan and spoon off fat. Add salt and pepper to taste.

7. Transfer stew to a serving bowl, sprinkle with parsley, and serve.

¼ cup olive oil

1¼ pounds stew beef, cut into 1-inch pieces

6 large cloves garlic, minced

5 cups demi-glace*

1 tablespoon Worcestershire sauce

1 cup Guinness beer

2 bay leaves

2 tablespoons butter

4 medium red potatoes, peeled and cut into ½-inch pieces

1 large onion, chopped

2 cups ½-inch pieces peeled carrots

Salt and freshly ground black pepper

Parsley for garnish

*Demi-glace can be found ready-made at your grocery or specialty store.

barcelona

executive chef | Michael Hazen

When too many dishes look tempting on the menu, choosing an appetizer and entree can prove taxing. At Barcelona, a restaurant and wine bar, the menu is extensive, but the decisions are easier. A bevy of tapas allows a small taste of many preparations. A tapas and salad sampler, meant to be shared, serves as a multiflavor prelude to a *plato principal*.

That kind of noshing can kick up a thirst. Barcelona covers the beverage category quite nicely with an extensive wine list of American and international wines, including about twenty-five vintages by the glass, as well as sherries, cocktails, and beer.

One of five locations in Connecticut, the busy New Haven outpost serves a menu similar to that of its Fairfield County and West Hartford locations. Executive chef Michael Hazen oversees the kitchen as well as a twenty-person chef's table, special tasting events, and cooking classes.

The sophisticated dining spaces boast some impressive design elements: a two-thousand-bottle chilled wine cellar and a dramatic thirty-foot mural of a Spanish bullfighter.

155 Temple St. | 203.848.3000
barcelonawinebar.com

Chickpea Puree
with Toasted Pita Chips

1. Preheat the oven to 350°F. On a jelly roll pan, spread the chickpeas in a single layer. You may need two pans. Sprinkle the scallions, shallots, and cilantro over the chickpeas and roast for about 15 minutes or until chickpeas are dry and the scallions and cilantro darken. Let the mixture cool in the pans.

2. Transfer the chickpeas to the bowl of a food processor fitted with a metal blade. Add the cream, tahini, cumin, and salt.

3. Cook the lemon in the microwave on high power for 15 seconds. Roll the lemon on the countertop under your palm to release the juices inside the lemon, and then slice it in half. Squeeze the juice from the lemon, strain out the seeds, and add to food processor.

4. Process the chickpea mixture until smooth. Taste and add salt if necessary. Scrape the puree from the bowl and set aside to cool to room temperature. Serve immediately upon cooling. If not ready to serve, put the puree in a container with a tight-fitting lid and refrigerate for up to 4 days. The puree can be served chilled or at room temperature.

5. When ready to serve, mound the chickpea puree in the center of a serving bowl. Arrange the pita chips in the puree by inserting their long sides into the base of the mound. Garnish with chopped scallions and serve.

2 15-ounce cans chickpeas, drained

6 scallions, white and green parts, coarsely chopped, plus ¼ cup chopped scallions for garnish

4 shallots, coarsely chopped

1 bunch cilantro, thick stems removed and discarded, leaves and some stems chopped

¾ cup heavy cream

⅓ cup tahini

3 teaspoons ground cumin

½ teaspoon salt, or more to taste

1 lemon

Cumin-Toasted Pita Chips (see recipe on facing page)

Cumin-Toasted Pita Chips

1. Preheat the oven to 425°F. Slice each pita bread in half and cut each half into 3 triangles for a total of 6 per pita.

2. Drizzle the pita triangles with about $3/4$ cup olive oil. Season the triangles with cumin and salt. Rub the seasonings onto the chips with one hand while tossing them with the other.

3. Spread the remaining $1/2$ cup olive oil in the bottom of two jelly roll or shallow baking pans so the oil covers them evenly and fully. Lay the pita triangles in an even layer on the pans.

4. Toast the chips for 12 to 14 minutes or until honey brown and crisp. Turn with a spatula and rotate the pans several times to encourage even browning and crisping. Transfer the chips to racks to cool. Once cool, serve immediately or store in a container with a tight-fitting lid for up to 3 days.

1 12-ounce package pita bread with pockets

1¼ cups olive oil

½ cup ground cumin

2 tablespoons kosher salt

the family table

by TODD LYON

Don't let the statistics fool you: On paper, New Haven is a medium-size city, population about 130,000. But in real life, as anyone who lives here will attest, New Haven is a small town. It's a place built on relationships—neighbors, friends, customers, families. With seven colleges and universities in our county, there's a mighty student population that comes and goes, but New Haven's full-timers tend to stay entrenched, to grow deep roots, and to remain close via strands of connectivity. Some connections are wispy and accidental; others are powerful enough to build dynasties.

This is also true with our city's most venerable restaurants. Many have family at the core, and most of those families arrived on our shores as immigrants who brought a sense of home to a strange new land via cookery—the flavors and aromas of the places they left behind. Generations of hard-working parents have reared children here whose "chores" included bussing tables and filling water glasses, and who in turn became chefs, managers, and servers, with children of their own who keep the family business strong.

Consider the story of Consiglio's restaurant. Originally called the Big Apple, it was established in 1938 by Annunziata and Salvatore Consiglio, natives of Amalfi, as a neighborhood tavern, feeding the working class on Wooster Street with plates of homemade cavatelli, braciola, or whatever Mama Annunziata decided to cook that day. The couple's nine children helped run the place, and today their offspring continue to lovingly operate Consiglio's, a glowing, white-tablecloth restaurant located across the street from where the Big Apple once stood.

Granddaughter Trish Consiglio-Perrotti is now at the helm; she and her sister Laura Fantarella represent the third generation of Consiglios. Dad Pasqual and Aunt Marie continue to work there every day, while Trish's kids—ten-year-old Matthew, eight-year-old Jason, and four-year-old Mia—love visiting the restaurant and helping out. (Matthew greets guests, hands out menus, and brings bread ("Like a mini maître d'," says Trish), while Jason loves washing dishes. Seeing the little ones in action is quite a thrill for Consiglio's long-time customers, some of whom have been patrons for forty-plus years and remember a time when Aunt Anna, waiting tables, wouldn't let anybody order meat on Fridays—even if they were Jewish.

Much of the menu at Consiglio's has been modernized over the years, and the restaurant has evolved into a fine dining establishment representing contemporary Italian cuisine. Yet the old dishes are always available, unchanged by time. Cavatelli, for instance, is still made fresh every day, the fresh pasta dough curled into tiny shells with the edge of a fork, while traditional Sunday suppers still satisfy families with slow-cooked meats and red sauces, much as they did more than seventy years ago.

■ ■ ■

Miya's Sushi, across town on Howe Street, has a similar story, but its cuisine was inspired by a very different part of the world.

Miya's saga started in the 1970s, when the lovely Yoshiko Lai, a native of Japan, and her Hong Kong–born

Trish Consiglio-Perrotti

husband, surgeon-researcher Yin-Lok Lai, were settling into a tiny apartment on Prospect Street with their young family. There, Yoshi, as she's known, started cooking specialties from her native land, with an emphasis on healthy eating (she earned a degree in nutrition in Japan). Japanese cuisine was entirely exotic to most New Englanders in those days, while coveted by other émigrés, and news of Yoshi's cookery spread until she found herself with a small catering business.

In 1982 Yoshi opened Miya's (named for her baby daughter) on Chapel Street, the first sushi bar in New Haven, and possibly all of Connecticut. A true pioneer, she not only fed her homesick countrymen but also introduced thousands of locals to the delights of raw toro, glistening tobiko, and perfect rolls wrapped in nori, to be delicately dipped in soy sauce and wasabi.

Her son, Bun Lai, a renaissance boy turned renaissance man, studied international relations with kindly Jesuits and then took to the road, tasting the world before returning to Connecticut in the early 1990s to get busy in his mother's kitchen.

Today Bun is leading a sushi revolution of sorts at Miya's on Howe Street, reinventing the form to reflect world cuisines and global sensibilities. "Food must be idealistic and romantic," muses Bun, who creates what he calls "cross-cultural sushi," borrowing techniques and ingredients from unexpected places like France and Mexico, not to mention his own backyard, where he forages indigenous edibles and turns them into bite-size works of art (and house-infused sakes).

Chef Bun is a rising culinary star and has been collecting awards and accolades at a dizzying pace, but success hasn't spoiled him: Miya's is still a low-key spot with ultra-personal service where budget-minded wanderers can down a beer and a roll at the bar (granted, Bun's creations have names like Sweet-Natured Kabuki Girl Roll and the Crab and His Mother, but many are hard to resist and all are extra delicious). Spenders with a sense of adventure can treat themselves to one of Bun's evening-length Kaiseki dinners, including course after course of madly inventive dishes, many of which are unrecognizable as sushi, and each has a story to tell.

And yes, Yoshi is still there, the spiritual center of the place, spreading love and blessings to one and all.

Steps away from Miya's Sushi is another New Haven institution: Mamoun's Falafel. Launched in Greenwich Village in 1971, Mamoun's was one of the first Middle Eastern eateries in the United States and remains the oldest falafel restaurant in New York City. So it follows that when Mamoun Chater opened his second location in New Haven in 1977, the concept of falafel, baba ghanoush, and shawarma were alien to most area diners.

But the burgeoning vegetarian population responded immediately, as did legions of students looking for satisfying, inexpensive fare. The fact that Mamoun's was (and still is) open until 3:00 a.m., 365 days a year, has definitely helped; insomniacs and night owls always had a place to go, as did those who found themselves far from home on the holidays. (Thanksgiving is one of Mamoun's busiest days of the year.)

While "Uncle Mamoun," as he's known, concentrated on the New York operations (in the 1980s another branch opened in Albany, and, a few years ago, a fourth location premiered in the East Village), the New Haven shop was watched over by Muhammad Chater, Mamoun's brother. It was he who kept Mamoun's—with its dark walls, mysterious lighting, and vigorous houseplants—a welcoming oasis for decades. Now that job falls to his son, Suleiman Chater, who, at forty, is wholly dedicated to carrying on his family's traditions. (While Mamoun is still with us, and lives in New Jersey, sadly, Muhammad passed away in 2006.)

How many hours per week does Suleiman log at the restaurant that is open twice as often as it's closed? He won't say. "It's a family business," he shrugs. "You're here when you need to be, and sometimes that's nonstop. But it's okay, because the customers are awesome."

• • •

If you don't believe that New Haven is a small town in which virtually everyone is interconnected, know that Bun Lai and Suleiman Chater are good friends who have an ongoing "who's more handsome" contest; Suleiman has influenced Bun's cookery, while Bun covered Mamoun's kitchen during

birth of the burger

Long credited with inventing the hamburger about one hundred years ago, Louis Lunch, a snug little cottage of a restaurant in downtown New Haven, still sends patties sizzling along on an ancient vertical grill to be served on white toast. Without ketchup—ever. Tomato and onion slices are allowed, and the potato salad is recommended. Eccentric and often erratic, Louis is all about the experience, so relax, take it all in, and enjoy a bite of juicy history.

Louis Lunch
263 Crown St. | 203.562.5507

Muhammad's funeral (the family decided that Dad wouldn't have wanted to close the place). Trish Consiglio-Perrotti, for her part, had her first date with her college sweetheart at Miya's, where she proceeded to fall "madly in love"; at around the same time, Bun took his high school girlfriend, whom he was equally crazy about, to dinner at Consiglio's.

In New Haven, no restaurant is an island, nor are the patrons who dine there.

Consiglio's
165 Wooster St. | 203.865.4489

Miya's Sushi
68 Howe St. | 203.777.9760

Mamoun's Falafel
85 Howe St. | 203.562.8444

the scoop meets the spatula

The antidote for trendy upstart restaurants in the Elm City is surely Clark's Dairy, a family-run, Formica-counter eatery that has been serving up doggedly traditional American fare for decades. Burgers, sandwiches, fries, and other soothing selections are sweetened by sundaes and shakes in a space that time forgot. Think Pleasantville without the abstract paintings, and you're home.

Clark's Dairy
74 Whitney Ave. | 203.777.2728

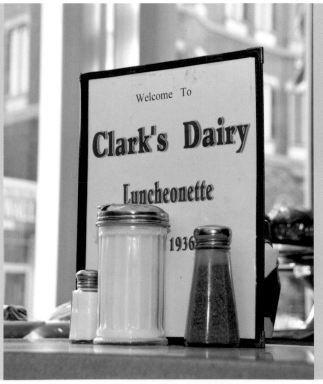

bespoke

executive chef | Yousef Ghalaini

Arturo and Suzette Franco-Camacho were key players in New Haven's hip restaurant scene, responsible for the popular Roomba, Bespoke, and Sabor. The couple traded New Haven for Branford just as 2009 closed, but they left the monumental Bespoke in capable hands.

New owner Lauren Kendzierski, who has degrees in culinary journalism, pastry, and business management, embraced Arturos and Suzette's vision. "It's just a great fit," she says. "It's my style of restaurant." She is putting her stamp on the trilevel space. A Bespoke sign on the contemporary glass-and-wood exterior directs guests inside. The restaurant remains open for dinner and late-night drinks and nibbles, but it now also serves lunch.

Lauren and executive chef Yousef Ghalaini, who met while working for Hartford's Max Restaurant Group, took the menu in a Modern American direction. Yousef, who is Lebanese, adds Mediterranean and Middle Eastern touches and counts on farm-fresh ingredients. "We are using as many local and sustainably sourced items as we can, from paper goods to food," Lauren says.

By the way, save room for dessert. When she is not tending to the business of running the restaurant, Lauren also is the pastry chef.

266 College St. | 203.562.4644
bespokenewhaven.com

Ricotta Cheesecake

SERVES 12–16

How lucky are we to have this delectable recipe for our very own? Extremely!
Thank you, Lauren.

2 pounds cream cheese, room temperature

1 cup sugar

4 egg yolks

2 eggs

½ teaspoon cinnamon

1 teaspoon grated orange zest

1 tablespoon rose water

1 quart ricotta cheese (get the real stuff from an Italian store or cheese market)

Fresh whipped cream for garnish (optional)

Candied orange peels for garnish (optional)

Organic rose petals for garnish (optional)

1. Preheat the oven to 275°F. Line the outside of a 10-inch springform pan with foil, all the way up the sides. Place the pan in a 2-inch-deep baking dish.

2. Place the cream cheese and sugar in the bowl of a stand mixer fitted with the paddle attachment; slowly beat the cream cheese with the sugar. You do not want to incorporate air into the batter, so go slow and steady. Continually wipe down the sides of the bowl with a rubber spatula. Add each yolk and egg, one at a time, and stir until incorporated. Add the cinnamon, orange zest, and rose water; stir. Remove bowl from machine.

3. By hand, break up the ricotta into the batter and use a spatula to fold everything together. Pour into the pan.

4. Pour warm water into the baking dish 1 inch up the sides of the springform pan. Bake until the center jiggles slightly and is no longer wet to the touch, about 1 hour.

5. Let cheesecake come to room temperature, cover, and then chill in the refrigerator for at least 2 hours.

6. Serve with fresh whipped cream, candied orange peels, and organic rose petals, if desired.

Salmon and Tuna Tartare

Though surprisingly easy to make, this dish is sure to dazzle. Use the freshest tuna for the best results.

1 round pita bread

1 tablespoon zaatar*

1 tablespoon sumac*

8 ounces sushi-grade yellowfin or bluefin tuna, skin removed by fishmonger

8 ounces wild king salmon or organic Scottish salmon, skin removed by fishmonger

1 scallion, thinly sliced

1 shallot, minced

¼ cup Spanish extra-virgin olive oil

½ cup freshly squeezed lemon juice

Salt and freshly ground black pepper

1 cup Greek yogurt or organic plain yogurt

Chive blossoms for garnish, if available

Zaatar and sumac are Middle Eastern spices can be found at most specialty grocery stores.

1. Preheat the oven to 350°F. Split the pita in half and then cut into random-shaped triangles, place on a baking sheet, and bake until golden brown, about 15–20 minutes. Immediately upon removing from the oven, sprinkle with half the zaatar and half the sumac and let cool.

2. Remove the dark bloodline from the skin side of both types of fish and dice into ¼-inch pieces. In a cold mixing bowl combine the fish, scallion, shallot, about ⅔ of the olive oil, and the lemon juice. Season with salt and pepper and set aside.

3. In another bowl, combine the yogurt and the remainder of the zaatar, sumac, and olive oil, and adjust the seasoning with a little salt.

4. To plate, spread the yogurt on a chilled platter using a spoon, arrange the fish mixture across the center, garnish with the chive blossoms, and serve the toasted pita chips on the side.

the blue pearl

executive chef | Conley Taylor

Reviewers have compared the Blue Pearl to hip cocktail lounges in New York City and Miami. The soft lighting, airy white decor, and relaxed atmosphere set the stage for cocktails, seasonal dishes, and food to share.

The dining room is open for dinner, but the evening doesn't end at the close of dinner service. When the rush is over, partying begins in the lounge with music and a late-night menu "that extends into the wee hours," says executive chef Conley Taylor.

Conley, a Southerner by birth, excels in American dishes with a Southern twist. To create his seasonal menus, he works closely with the bar manager to develop dishes that complement the changing selection of cocktails and wines.

The Blue Pearl can offer a romantic dinner for two or shared plates for a party of eight. A signature offering is a variety of savory or sweet fondues, a fun way to eat. "It's a nice thing to sit around and share and create a sense of camaraderie," Conley says.

130 Court St. | 203.789.6370
thebluepearlnewhaven.com

Steamed Clams with Chorizo

SERVES 2

Quick, easy, and using just one pan, what could better than delicious New England clams made right at home? This robust dish is perfect served over your favorite pasta or rice, or you can enjoy its full flavor with toasted crusty bread perfect for dipping into the lovely broth.

1 tablespoon olive oil

1 tablespoon minced garlic

1 tablespoon minced shallot

1 link chorizo sausage, sliced

1 dozen littleneck clams, rinsed well to remove sand and grit

½ cup white wine

¼ cup diced tomatoes

Juice from half a lime

1 tablespoon chopped cilantro

1 tablespoon chopped scallions

Salt and freshly ground black pepper

1. Heat the olive oil in a medium saucepan over medium-high heat for about a minute. Add garlic and shallot and sear until lightly brown. Add chorizo, clams, white wine, and tomatoes and cover. Simmer for 10 minutes or until clams open.

2. Remove from heat and finish with lime juice, cilantro, and scallions. Add salt and pepper to taste.

Glen Rosengrant, Gabriel Morris, and Chris Mordecai

café romeo

executive chef | Chris Mordecai

Nestled in the heart of the East Rock neighborhood is this sleek, modern cafe with a friendly staff, terrific menu, and reasonable prices. Co-owner Chris Mordecai, who lives on Orange Street, says he opened the restaurant because "East Rock had everything but a good cup of coffee."

In addition to organic, fair-trade java, Café Romeo turns out personal pizzas from a gas-fired stone oven, hearty soups and sandwiches, entree salads, breakfast dishes, and baked goods, all made from scratch. The menu is updated Italian, using locally produced ingredients. "We tried to keep Old World Italy but with an urban flair," he says.

Like the neighborhood, the clientele is a mix of Yale students, families, and professionals from nearby offices. Chris, who left a job at the phone company, couldn't be happier in his new career. "There's definitely a community here," he says. "It's more work, double the hours, and more stress than working at AT&T, but it's fun and you meet so many nice people."

534 Orange St. | 203.865.2233
cafe-romeo.com

Sausage Frittata

Vegetable-oil cooking spray

1 pound Italian sausage

2 tablespoons unsalted butter

1 large Spanish onion, julienned

Salt and freshly ground black pepper

¼ cup white wine

¼ cup vegetable oil

3 small- to medium-size Yukon Gold potatoes, cut into medium dice

6 large cremini mushrooms, sliced

3 roasted red bell peppers (or 1 12-ounce jar roasted red peppers), julienned

12 jumbo eggs

½ cup heavy cream

½ pound provolone cheese, shredded

1½ cups ricotta cheese

6 grape tomatoes, sliced in half lengthwise

12 small sprigs fresh rosemary

1. Preheat the oven to 350°F. Thoroughly spray a muffin pan with vegetable-oil cooking spray.

2. Spray a 12-inch sauté pan with vegetable-oil cooking spray. Add the sausage and cook over medium-high heat for 5 minutes; turn the heat down to medium and simmer for 5 more minutes. Turn the sausage over and cook until sausage is golden brown and tender, about 8 more minutes. Remove from heat and let cool. Dice the sausage.

3. In the 12-inch sauté pan over medium-low heat, melt the butter. Add the onion and a pinch of salt and pepper and turn the heat up to medium-high. Cook, stirring occasionally, until the onions reach a deep brown caramel color. Add the wine and cook, stirring continuously, until most of the liquid has evaporated. Remove from heat and let cool.

4. Heat the vegetable oil in another sauté pan over medium-high heat until barely smoking, about 2 minutes. Add potatoes and a pinch of salt and pepper. Cook evenly on all sides until golden brown. Remove from heat and let cool.

5. Evenly distribute mushrooms, onions, roasted red peppers, potatoes, and sausage among the 12 muffin cups in the pan.

6. Beat the eggs, cream, and a pinch of salt and pepper until the eggs are evenly colored and textured. Evenly distribute the eggs among the muffin cups as well. Evenly distribute the provolone cheese among the tops of the cups.

7. Bake for 20 to 25 minutes, or until the eggs have puffed up and the tops are golden brown (a toothpick inserted in the center of one of the cups should come out dry). Allow the frittatas to cool for 5 minutes, then carefully remove them from the pan without inverting it.

8. Garnish with a quenelle of ricotta cheese, half a grape tomato, and a sprig of fresh rosemary.

Cranberry Curry Scone

MAKES 8 SINGLE-SERVE SCONES

[Recipe courtesy Gabriel Morris]

What could be better than a warm, fresh-baked scone and tea or coffee while passing the hours at your favorite cafe? Café Romeo makes this lovely melt-in-your-mouth delight with sour cherries and curry.

1. Preheat the oven to 375°F. Line a sheet pan with parchment paper. In a large mixing bowl sift together flour, sugar, baking powder, baking soda, curry powder, and salt.

2. Cut butter into the dry ingredients with a pastry cutter or two knives. Butter should begin to form pea-size balls.

3. In a small bowl, whisk 1 egg into the heavy cream and add to the flour mixture; stir to combine. The dough will have a shaggy consistency. You may add a little extra cream, but don't wet the mixture too much. Add the cranberries.

4. Form dough into a disk about 1 inch thick and cut it into 8 triangles. Place the triangles on prepared sheet pan.

5. In a small bowl whisk together 1 egg and 1 teaspoon water. Brush the top of each scone with the egg wash.

6. Bake until golden brown, 18 to 20 minutes.

4 cups cake flour

½ cup sugar

1 tablespoon baking powder

1 teaspoon baking soda

2 tablespoons curry powder

½ teaspoon salt

1½ sticks (12 tablespoons) cold butter, cut into small cubes

2 large eggs

1½ cups heavy cream

½ cup dried cranberries

1 teaspoon water

from seed,
growing community

by JAN ELLEN SPIEGEL

The center of New Haven's foodie universe may well be an unassuming block-long street between Wooster and Chapel in the heart of the Little Italy neighborhood. On Saturday mornings, the block—DePalma Court—is transformed into the Wooster Square farmers' market, the flagship of four markets run by the non-profit CitySeed.

Since it began in 2004, the market has blossomed into the premiere market in the state, with more than two dozen vendors and a waiting list, and CitySeed has become the state's model for market systems and how to connect urban residents with fresh, local, and affordable food.

They do indeed, but in the heart of the summer produce season—that's when they really come out. It is the place to be on Saturdays from 9 a.m. to 1 p.m. with wall-to-wall shoppers, kids, and dogs sampling the startling array of all that is fresh and local in Connecticut—including doggie treats.

The food choices are overwhelming and it takes almost no effort to buy way more than you need. Arugula is everywhere, but the greens wander into the unusual, including Zemelsky's giant red mustard, Tokyo bekana, ruby streaks, and Bordeaux spinach; the esoteric hydroponic offerings from Two Guys From Woodbridge; and unusual head lettuces from Yale Farm—this market is its only public outlet.

There are tomatoes from organic to heirloom to just plain old round red. All manner of vegetables, from the usual to the oddball. Trinity Dairy brings its milk, yogurt, and fresh butter all the way from Enfield. Rose's Berry Farm comes with its Connecticut River Valley berries and tree fruit. There are meat, eggs, chicken for the ordering, shellfish, bread, baked goods, cheeses.

Stacia and Fred Monahan of Stone Gardens in Shelton are especially happy about the producer-only mandate. "I want to sell with other real farmers who are actually growing everything that they're selling at the markets," Stacia says.

But as important as the food is, the CitySeed markets are as much about atching up with friends and making new ones as they are about doing weekly food shopping.

And that's pretty much what the four founding neighbors had in mind when they started the whole thing, looking to get something other than pizza into their neighborhood.

"It was always about access—connecting urban residents with fresh healthy farm food," explains Jennifer McTiernan, CitySeed cofounder and former executive director. But it was also always about the city. "The markets in New Haven create this sense of community. They prompt neighborhood revitalization; they prompt people to hang out. There's this sense of growing community and engaging the community," McTiernan says. "What I think is so amazing about the market is that it's the place you go to get the best food."

It is also affordable. Each market accepts food stamps, WIC, and senior market coupons. CitySeed provides demonstrations, recipe cards, a bilingual cookbook, and newsletters with information on how to use what it sells. And there are a host of programs that bring fresh local food directly to low-income people and workplaces and teach children as young as preschool age about fresh food.

"They're the best run farmers' market organization in the state," says Rick Macsuga of the Connecticut Department of Agriculture, who oversees the 100-plus farmers' markets in Connecticut. "The whole concept of connecting the farmers' market to the whole food system was an important concept that spread through the state."

The outreach and advertising done by CitySeed creates a vibrant marketplace that attracts a diverse array of market-goers. This professional management allows farmers to focus on bringing the best products to market and building relationships with customers. These direct-to-consumer opportunities are vital in supporting successful farming ventures.

It's one of the reasons Patrick Horan drives all the way from Washington, Connecticut with certified organic tomatoes and other produce from his Waldingfield Farm. Another: "We get five times the amount of foot traffic as other markets," he says. And on top of that: "There's an altruistic aspect of what CitySeed's mission is. We agree with it."

With a mission to engage the community in growing an equitable, local food system that promotes economic development, community development and sustainable agriculture, CitySeed is present in many areas of the food system.

The organization has helped growers link to restaurants in search of local food and schools that are trying to feed their students better-quality meals, and it has in general sparked a local food awareness in New Haven that never existed before.

McTiernan says simply: "This is about changing the food culture in New Haven." No question, CitySeed is accomplishing that.

cityseed.org

shake the hand
that feeds you.
—MICHAEL POLLAN

carmen anthony steakhouse

executive chef | Walid Gad

Waterbury native Carmen Anthony Vacalebre has come a long way from a degree in "Hamburgerology" from McDonald's University. After thirty-plus years in the fast-food industry, he made the leap from franchises to white-tablecloth restaurants when he opened the first Carmen Anthony Steakhouse in Waterbury in May 1996. The entrepreneur now reigns over a statewide empire of stylish restaurants specializing in fresh fish and Black Angus beef.

Vacalebre's New Haven chophouse opened in 2004. In the bar, where Angus burgers and prime rib sandwiches are on the menu, a floor-to-ceiling window allows guests to keep tabs on the street life in this up-and-coming business neighborhood.

In the handsome dining room, beef is king, with filet mignon, porterhouse, ribeye, and strip steaks grilled to order. Specialty dishes such as filet mignon topped with lobster meat and a Gorgonzola demi-glace reflect Vacalebre's Italian heritage.

In addition to a wine list recognized by the prestigious *Wine Spectator* magazine, the restaurant offers a private wine locker program. Customers can purchase fine wines at a discount and store them in lockers identified by brass plates with the owners' names.

660 State St. | 203.773.1444
carmenanthonyrestaurant.com

Chicken Carmen Anthony

A classic favorite at Carmen Anthony Steakhouse, fresh boneless chicken breasts, breaded and sautéed and covered with a garlic beurre blanc sauce, are sure to become a forever specialty at your home as well. Serve with rice or potatoes and a side of fresh sautéed vegetables.

For the chicken:

Salt and freshly ground black pepper

2 6-ounce boneless chicken breasts

1 cup all-purpose flour

2 eggs, beaten

1 cup panko bread crumbs

2 tablespoons olive oil

For the sauce:

1 tablespoon olive oil

½ tablespoon minced garlic

¾ cup white wine

1¼ cups heavy cream

1½ sticks (12 tablespoons) cold butter, cut into pieces

Salt and freshly ground black pepper

1. To prepare the chicken, preheat the oven to 350°F. Salt and pepper the chicken breasts on both sides. Place the flour on a plate, the eggs in a shallow bowl, and the bread crumbs on a plate. Place a chicken breast into the flour, coating both sides, then dip into the beaten eggs, then the bread crumbs, coating both sides each time. Shake off excess. Repeat for the remaining chicken breast.

2. Heat 2 tablespoons oil in a pan over medium-high heat. When hot, sear both sides of the chicken breasts until golden brown. Place breasts in a baking dish and bake until chicken is cooked through, about 25 minutes.

3. Meanwhile, prepare the sauce: Place a saucepan over medium heat until hot; add the oil. Add the garlic and white wine and cook until reduced by three-quarters, about 15–20 minutes.

4. Add the heavy cream and simmer over moderate heat until reduced by three-quarters. As it reduces, the cream will thicken slightly.

5. Stir in the butter a piece at a time, adding each piece before the previous one has completely melted. Lift the pan occasionally to cool the mixture. Sauce should not get hot enough to separate. Season with salt and pepper.

6. Place chicken breasts on plates and pour half of the sauce over each piece. Divide the remaining sauce into small ramekins for dipping.

Award-Winning Grilled Prime Rib SERVES 1

Carmen Anthony Steakhouse won Best Prime Rib in Connecticut in the *Connecticut Magazine* Reader's Poll, 2010! Now you can make this award-winner at home.

1. Preheat oven to 350°F. Place meat in a baking pan and cook in oven for 2 1/2 to 3 hours, depending on weight of rib.

2. Place ribeye on the grill and cook to desired temperature.

3. Season with Montreal Seasoning. Place steak on plate, ladle about 1/4 cup of au jus on top.

4. Serve with horseradish sauce.

1 16-ounce boneless ribeye

2 teaspoons Montreal Seasoning*

1/4 cup horseradish sauce, for serving

* Montreal Seasoning can be found in most markets and grocery stores.

CASEUS
FROMAGERIE • BISTRO
93 WHITNEY AVENUE, NEW HAVEN

ARTISAN CHEESE
CHARCUTERIE
SMALL PLATES
PRESERVES

OLIVE OILS
VINEGARS
WINE
BEER

EVERY CHEESE HAS A

Jason Sobocinski

caseus

executive chef | Joe D'Alesio

Caseus is the Latin word for "cheese," and the name signifies the most important ingredient at this quaint bistro and fromagerie. Owner and New Haven native Jason Sobocinski and his chef, Joe D'Alesio, search out locally grown and artisanal ingredients, including meats from heritage breeds and cheeses produced in Connecticut.

The menu changes at least four times a year, in keeping with the seasons, but certain "classics," including a grilled cheese sandwich like no other, are year-round staples. "Many of our signature dishes are classics made in a classical way with a little fun, with our own style," Jason says.

Armed with a graduate degree in gastronomy from Boston University, Jason opened Caseus in January 2008. A brick and wood-paneled bar on the street level serves as the main dining room, but there also are tables set in nooks and crannies downstairs on the way to the specialty food shop. An outdoor patio is open as weather permits.

"I just wanted to open a little cheese shop with a bistro and feed people good food—food that I like to eat," Jason says. Cheese aficionados, prepare to be wooed.

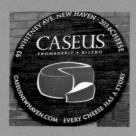

93 Whitney Ave. | 203.624.3373
caseusnewhaven.com

Beet and Chèvre Salad

Not only are they sweet in flavor, loaded with energy-enhancing vitamin B, and absolutely beautiful to look at, beets are a great regional vegetable available nearly year-round from local sources. The variety of color and taste suits both New England's harsh winters and sticky summers. This recipe is a great summertime version that uses a local goat's milk cheese from Lebanon, Connecticut. In the winter Caseus substitutes blue cheese from Cato Corner Farm in Colchester, Connecticut, for a heartier, more robust salad.

4 large (softball-size) beets

3 tablespoons peanut or canola oil

Salt and freshly ground black pepper

Juice of 2 lemons

¼ cup extra-virgin olive oil

Several handfuls of light greens such as mâche, watercress, arugula, tatsoi, or mizuna

¼ cup shelled pistachios, lightly toasted

6–8 ounces Beltane chèvre

Maldon sea salt*

Maldon salt is a flaky, delicious English sea salt.

1. Preheat the oven to 400°F. Wash beets under cold water and pat dry. Toss the beets with the oil and a bit of salt and pepper.

2. Place beets in a roasting pan or on a cookie sheet with sides, and roast in the oven for 1 hour, checking with the tip of a paring knife for doneness. (Different size beets will take more or less time, so stay on top of them.) If the knife goes into the beets easily and comes out quickly, the beets are done.

3. Remove the beets from the oven. While they are still hot, use a kitchen towel designated for beets (it will be purple after this procedure; you've been warned) to rub each beet until its skin is removed. Allow beets to cool, then rinse them under cold water. Cut the beets into slices or matchsticks and set aside.

4. Combine the lemon juice and olive oil and whisk vigorously until emulsified. This step can be done in a blender, but the dressing should look rustic and slightly separated. Season with salt and freshly ground black pepper.

5. Lightly toss the salad greens with the dressing. Place beets on the greens and sprinkle with pistachios. Finish with a light drizzle of the dressing over the beets, some crumbled pieces of the Beltane chèvre, and a pinch of Maldon sea salt.

Poutine

An after-hours staple in Montreal, this hearty dish is said to have been invented by Canadian truckers looking to take with them all the components of a perfect meal—cheese, gravy, and french fries—in a cup. Genius.

1. To prepare the sauce, melt the butter in a saucepan over medium heat. Stir in the flour and cook for several minutes, until the roux is thick and does not taste floury. Whisk in the stock and cream until smooth. Bring the liquid to a boil. Season with salt and pepper. Remove from the heat and set aside.

2. To prepare the french fries, heat the oil in a saucepan to 300°F (use a candy thermometer to measure the temperature).

3. Peel the potatoes and cut into $1/4$-inch-thick french fries. Rinse in cold water and drain thoroughly.

4. Blanch the potatoes in small batches in the hot oil until soft but not brown, 4 to 5 minutes.

5. Remove potatoes and let cool to room temperature. This step is best done ahead, as far as a few hours before eating.

6. When ready to serve, heat oil to 375°F to 400°F. Fry the blanched potatoes in small batches in the hot oil until lightly browned and crispy. Drain the hot fries on newspaper or brown paper bags. Season with salt and pepper.

7. Break the cheese curds into 1-inch pieces and place them into cups. Reheat the velouté sauce, stirring, to a slow simmer. Put hot fries into the cups to cover the cheese curds. Fries should be sticking out of the cups. Finish each cup with a healthy dose of the velouté.

For the velouté (gravy):

3 tablespoons unsalted butter

3 tablespoons all-purpose flour

2 cups chicken stock

1 cup heavy cream

Salt and freshly ground black pepper

For the pommes frites (french fries):

2 quarts or more peanut oil

8 large Idaho potatoes

Salt and freshly ground black pepper

½ pound fresh cheese curds*

Paper cups (thick enough for coffee but not Styrofoam)

*Caseus uses Calabro mozzarella curds, but mail-order Wisconsin curds are the best for this recipe, and their great traditional squeaky quality is worth the extra planning required.

christopher martins

executive chef | Brian Virtue

Christopher Martins is two restaurants in one. On one side is a Cheers-like two-level bar and pub, while a more intimate dining room occupies the other side of the restaurant. Brian Virtue, a Culinary Institute of America–trained chef and co-owner with Chris Vigilante, describes the food as "American bistro leaning towards Italian." The pub menu is as it should be: lots of finger-licking appetizers as well as interesting salads and hearty sandwiches. The restaurant menu's offerings reflect the more formal aspect of the white-tablecloth dining room.

Yet Christopher Martins's guests can choose what they want to eat and where they want to eat it. "They get to live both lifestyles," Brian says. "They can get a good burger in a quiet setting or a veal chop in a pub setting."

Those customers also dine on dishes made from local ingredients. Brian and Chris give back to the community in ways beyond supporting local farmers and food producers. They serve Thanksgiving Day dinner to those in need, they host changing exhibits of local artists' work in the dining room, and they sponsor a Christmas race to collect toys for children.

860 State St. | 203.776.8835
christophermartins.com

Scallops Wrapped in Pancetta over Wilted Arugula

SERVES 4

This dish is a twist on the old scallops and bacon classic. Using pancetta instead of bacon adds a more delicate, less smoky flavor to the dish and complements the scallops better. This can be served as a passed hors d'oeuvre, as an appetizer (in a smaller portion), or as an entree. Christopher Martins has done similar dishes substituting shrimp for the sea scallops and adding some fontina cheese while wrapping the shrimp.

20 large sea scallops

20 slices pancetta

Extra-virgin olive oil for sautéing

4 cloves garlic

2 pounds arugula, cleaned and stemmed

1½ cups white wine

1 tablespoon Dijon mustard

Juice of 2 lemons

4 tablespoons (½ stick) butter

1. Wrap each scallop with a slice of pancetta.

2. Heat olive oil in large sauté pan over high heat. Add wrapped scallops and sauté on both sides until browned. Remove from pan and set aside in a warm spot.

3. Add garlic and sauté until brown. Add arugula and cook just until wilted.

4. Place wilted arugula on plates and top with scallops.

5. Add white wine to pan to deglaze. Stir in mustard, lemon juice, and butter and stir until sauce comes together. Spoon over top of scallops and serve.

> A glass of white Burgundy, maybe a Pouilly-Fuissé, goes extraordinarily well with this dish.
>
> —BRIAN VIRTUE

Thai Sirloin-Wrapped Asparagus

This is a great summer dish, because you get a mix of hot and cold, spicy and sweet. The grilled beef marinade is spicy hot, but it is balanced nicely with the cold sweetness of the citrus dressing on the jicama slaw, which has a great crunchiness to contrast with the asparagus.

1. To prepare the vinaigrette, combine the juices, honey, and shallot. Whisk in canola oil, cilantro, salt, and pepper.

2. To prepare the jicama slaw, combine all ingredients and toss with vinagrette to coat.

3. To prepare the Thai marinade, place all ingredients in a food processor and puree until smooth.

4. Brush sliced beef with Thai marinade. Wrap marinated beef around pieces of asparagus and grill for 4 to 5 minutes, turning as necessary to avoid burning.

5. Place a portion of jicama slaw in the center of each plate and surround it with the grilled beef and asparagus.

For the citrus vinaigrette:

Juice of 1 lemon

Juice of 1 lime

Juice of 1 orange

2 tablespoons honey

1 shallot, minced

1 cup canola oil

2 tablespoons chopped cilantro

Salt and freshly ground black pepper

For the jicama slaw:

1 pound jicama, julienned

½ red bell pepper, julienned

For the Thai marinade:

¼ cup peanut butter

1 tablespoon honey

1 tablespoon spicy mustard

1 teaspoon cayenne pepper

½ bunch cilantro, chopped

1 teaspoon minced fresh ginger

1 teaspoon minced fresh garlic

For the beef and asparagus:

12 1-ounce pieces New York sirloin, sliced paper thin

12 medium to large pieces asparagus

claire's corner copia
& basta trattoria

executive chefs | Claire Criscuolo, Frank Criscuolo & Daniel Sergi

Just steps away from the main Yale campus, Claire's Corner Copia is a home away from home for students who crave a nourishing vegetarian meal in a laid-back atmosphere. The restaurant, open since 1975, draws the city's worker bees as well, with its eclectic mix of hearty Mexican specialties and breakfast dishes, veggie burgers, pizzas, sandwiches, and salads.

Next door is Claire's sibling, Basta Trattoria, which opened on New Year's Eve in 2004. Its brick walls, hardwood floors, open kitchen, and wood-fired oven are reminiscent of the small, family-owned eateries that Claire and Frank Criscuolo frequent on their trips to Italy. Here, with chef Daniel Sergi overseeing the kitchen, the menu is strictly Italian, but in both of the Criscuolos' restaurants, the emphasis is on local, organic, and sustainable ingredients.

The two restaurants let this dynamic duo not only interact with their guests but also give back to the community. Claire Criscuolo works with the Growing Connection, a United Nations–sponsored program that teaches schoolchildren how to grow food. Claire's Corner Copia donates 10 percent of its profits to charity, while both restaurants frequently sponsor special dinners and events to benefit causes and nonprofit groups.

Claire's Corner Copia
1000 Chapel St. | 203.562.3888
clairescornercopia.com

Basta Trattoria
1006 Chapel St. | 203.772.1715
bastatrattoria.com

Golden Beet Salad

[Claire's Corner Copia]

Golden beets are grown locally from July through mid-October, and you should take advantage of their freshness during those months for peak flavor and also because it's important to support our local farmers. Golden beets have a sweet and mild flavor and a silky and smooth texture. This root vegetable is delicious and rich in iron and vitamins A and C.

Salt and freshly ground black pepper

2 large golden beets (about the size of large oranges), with greens

2 tablespoons grapeseed oil

1 tablespoon sherry wine vinegar syrup (see recipe below)

1 small red onion, cut into thin rings, separated

1. Bring a large pot of lightly salted water to a boil over high heat.

2. Wash the beets and greens under cold water to remove the sand and grit. Trim the beets to 2 inches above the base of the stems. Trim away and discard any brown leaves and the tough stems from the beet greens. Reserve the remaining leaves and tender stems. Wash the beets again, using your hands to rub off any remaining sand.

3. Cook the beets in the boiling water until they are just tender when pierced in the center with a fork, 20 to 45 minutes, depending on size.

4. Meanwhile, fill a bowl or the sink with cold water, scatter the beet greens in the water, and thoroughly wash them to remove any sand. Lift the greens out of the water. If there is any sand remaining in the bowl or sink, drain the water, and repeat until all the sand is removed. This second washing will ensure the removal of all the sand. Drain and coarsely chop the leaves and stems.

5. Bring a small pot of lightly salted water to a boil over high heat. Add the chopped greens and stir to cover the greens with the boiling water. Cook for 1 minute, until they wilt. Drain and turn into a small bowl.

6. In another small bowl, combine the grapeseed oil, sherry wine vinegar syrup, salt, and pepper, whisking to mix. Set aside.

7. When beets are tender, drain them and set aside until they are cool enough to handle. Use your fingers to remove the skin; it should peel off easily. Cut the beets into 1/4-inch slices.

8. Drizzle 1 tablespoon vinegar syrup mixture over the wilted greens and toss to coat, using your hands or tongs.

9. Arrange the greens on a platter. Arrange the sliced beets in the center of the platter, overlapping to form an attractive design. Scatter the onion rings evenly over the beets. Drizzle the remaining 2 tablespoons vinegar syrup mixture evenly over the beets.

Sherry Wine Vinegar Syrup

Heat 1/4 cup sherry wine vinegar in a heavy pot over low to medium heat. Cook at just below a simmer, swirling the pot every now and again, for about 7 minutes, until thickened and reduced to 1 tablespoon.

Butternut Squash Sauce with Local Sausages, Broccoli, and Organic Penne Pasta

SERVES 6

[Basta Trattoria]

The rich colors of this traditional Italian sauce remind us of the fall season in Amalfi. But this delicious and healthful dish, rich in beta carotene, vitamins A and C, and fiber, should be enjoyed during the late summer and winter months, too, when our local winter squash is at its peak flavor.

Olive oil spray

½ pound locally produced Italian sweet (or hot) sausage, in 1 or 2 links

¼ cup water

¼ cup organic extra-virgin olive oil

4 large cloves organic garlic, sliced

2 pounds butternut squash, peeled and cut into 1-inch slices

1 large organic sweet onion, cut into thick slices

¼ cup fresh organic basil leaves, cut in half lengthwise

½ cup coarsely chopped organic Italian flat-leaf parsley

Salt and freshly ground black pepper

1 pound organic whole-wheat or semolina penne pasta or other pasta

2 large broccoli crowns, separated into florets

⅛ teaspoon ground nutmeg

¼ cup lightly toasted pumpkin seeds (optional)

1. Preheat the oven to 400°F. Spray baking dish with olive oil.

2. Place the sausage into baking dish and pour water around, not over, the sausage. Bake for 12 to 15 minutes, or until the sausage is a medium brown and the center is a deep, dark pink (cut the sausage in half to check for doneness). Set aside until cool enough to handle, then cut the links into $^1/_2$-inch slices.

3. Heat oil in a large pot over medium-low heat. Add the garlic, squash, onion, basil, parsley, salt, and pepper. Stir to coat with the oil. Cover and cook, stirring occasionally, for about 25 minutes or until squash is just tender and has released some of its moisture.

4. Meanwhile, cook pasta according to package directions. One minute before draining, stir in broccoli florets. Before draining the pasta and broccoli, reserve 2 cups of the cooking water. (An easy way to remember this is to set a measuring cup into a colander set in the sink.)

5. When the squash is just tender, add the reserved pasta cooking water, the sausage, and the nutmeg. Stir well to mix. Cover and cook for about 5 minutes, stirring occasionally. Add pasta and broccoli florets to the pot and toss well. Taste for seasoning and adjust if necessary. Turn into a serving bowl. Top with the toasted pumpkin seeds if desired.

When you eat locally grown foods, the flavors will always be fresh and true to the Italian way of eating.

—CLAIRE CRISCUOLO

Basta chef Daniel Sergi

eats on
the street

by JAN ELLEN SPIEGEL

One of New Haven's best food deals, but probably also its best-kept secret, is its outdoor food carts.

On any given weekday at lunchtime there are about one hundred food carts on the streets, but unlike your basic big city hot dog and pretzel guys, New Haven's vendors are a United Nations of street food.

Indian, Thai, Chinese, Japanese, Vietnamese, Korean, Ethiopian, Moroccan, Mexican, Latino, Italian, Mediterranean, Middle Eastern—and you can still find a stray cart or two with hamburgers, hot dogs, and french fries. Much of the food is made fresh on the spot—stir-fried, griddled, grilled, and, occasionally, deep-fried. And it's cheap. You'd be hard-pressed to find anything that costs more than $6. Oh—and did we mention you can get all these choices in one place?

The carts tend to concentrate in three locations: about a half dozen along Long Wharf and another fifteen or so near the Peabody Museum. But the big draw is Cedar Street across from Yale–New Haven Hospital's main entrance, where you can find close to three dozen carts when the weather is good, not all that many less when it's lousy, and long lines always.

"This is one heck of a street," exclaims Keith Gavin, whose Bubba Gump hot dogs and knishes are relatively new to Cedar Street. "I worked in Manhattan down by the World Trade Center for years, but the food out here—it's second to none; it's really dynamite."

Bubba Gump is a food cart–only enterprise, but most of the vendors also have restaurants. Most notable among them are the four Tijuana Taco Company carts. They are part of chef Arturo Franco-Camacho's Nuevo Latino kingdom (Bespoke and Sabor). In fact the carts, which are mainly known for their burritos stuffed with Mexican-style pulled pork, black beans, and a caramelized onion and mushroom mixture, all with a dash of chipotle, began in 1996, years before the first of Arturo's restaurants—Roomba (now closed).

"It makes food accessible to people who can't afford to come down to the restaurant," says Suzette, Arturo's wife. "It shows food doesn't have to be expensive to be good."

Other restaurants, like Lalibela, an Ethiopian restaurant in New Haven, and Swagat, an Indian restaurant in West Haven, and restaurants as far away as Bridgeport, use the carts to bolster business at their sit-down places. Equally as important, the restaurants provide a location to do most of the food prep; there are some carts that bring everything cooked and just keep it hot.

Either way, the city keeps a tight quality-control lid on all the operators—no backyard barbecuers or recreational foodies. Most cart operators must take a class on proper health and safety for street vending, and all must buy yearly health department and vending licenses. The health department inspects the carts several times a year.

Most of the carts are just that—pushcarts that go on the sidewalk. But there are a few vending trucks with full kitchens. Giacomo's for one, with a spot staked out near the Peabody Museum, starts serving breakfast from its truck around 7:30 a.m. Owners Jack and Dawn DiNuzzo travel with a stove, grill, griddle, and warmer trays, and churn out eggs (their biggest seller), burgers, and grilled hot dogs until 2 p.m.

In the end, there's something for everyone, carnivore and vegetarian alike: any Chinese dish you can think of, Japanese udon noodles and soup, dumplings of all

nationalities, falafel, couscous and veggies, kimchee (for the true believers), curry of all kinds, California rolls, fresh *injera* with your Ethiopian collard greens or lentils, fresh pad thai or drunken noodles, and noodles, noodles, and more noodles stir-fried in front of you into just about anything. You can even find pasta alla vodka, cheesesteaks, and sausage-and-pepper subs. And if it's your pleasure, you can always find bottles of sriracha hot sauce.

foster's restaurant

executive chef | David Foster

The spare, clean lines of the wood and stone dining room, accented with punches of red, are the backdrop for what chef-owner David Foster calls his "eccentric American cuisine." "It's things you know, but we've taken them to a different level," he says. "We've deconstructed them and reconstructed them."

Dishes like ostrich and foie gras meatloaf with wild mushroom gravy and short ribs osso buco with ginger zinfandel sauce are familiar yet new. Fresh fish, seafood, game meats, and poultry are staples on the menu, while David also explores the world of wild boar, venison, turtle, and the like at special monthly dinners.

The 140-seat restaurant also features a lounge, bar, and private dining room. The granite-topped chef's table in the dining room allows the chef to assume the role of showman. Six guests can put their palates in his creative hands for a fourteen-course tasting menu and watch David whip up each dish at the six-burner gas stove. Expect the unexpected: "We like to stretch our wings and see how far we can take it."

56 Orange St. | 203.859.6666
fostersrestaurant.com

Herb-Crusted Petite Filet with Mango and Roasted Corn Salsa

Delicious and beautiful in its presentation, this savory dish will surely delight everyone at your table.

For the salsa:

3 ears of corn

2 ripe mangos

1 jalapeño, minced

3 tablespoons diced red bell pepper

Salt and freshly ground black pepper

¼ cup chopped fresh cilantro

3 tablespoons olive oil

For the filet:

3 pounds cleaned filet mignon, cut into 6
   equal portions

Salt and freshly ground black pepper

3 tablespoons chopped fresh rosemary

3 tablespoons chopped fresh thyme

3 tablespoons chopped fresh basil

2 tablespoons olive oil

1. Husk corn and grill until done and lightly charred. Cut kernels off the cob.

2. Peel 1 mango then cut it into small dice; set aside.

3. Peel the second mango and cut into chunks; add it to a blender and puree. It is all right for the mango puree to be slightly lumpy.

4. Place the corn, diced mango, mango puree, both peppers, salt and pepper, cilantro, and olive oil in a mixing bowl and mix well. Set aside.

5. To prepare the steak, season filets with salt and pepper.

6. In a dish or on a small plate, mix the chopped rosemary, thyme, and basil. Dredge each filet in the fresh herb mixture.

7. Heat the olive oil in a sauté pan over medium-high heat. Place filets in the oil, being very careful not to splash the oil. Cook to the temperature and doneness desired.

8. Plate each filet and top with a good-size spoonful of the salsa.

Green Tea–Marinated Bay Scallop Skewers with Ginger Cilantro Sauce

Scallops take on an Asian twist with this wonderful combination of flavors.

1. To prepare the marinade, combine the green tea powder, sesame oil, garlic, lime juice and zest, and salt and pepper in a small bowl.

2. Add the scallops and toss gently. Let sit for at least 20 minutes. This step can also be done earlier in the day or the night before.

3. Place about five marinated scallops on each bamboo skewer. Set aside.

4. To prepare the dipping sauce, place the mayonnaise, honey, sesame oil, soy sauce, ginger, and cilantro in a small bowl. Mix well and taste for additional salt or pepper. Divide evenly among 4 small ramekins for individual dipping, or pour into one large bowl for group dipping.

5. To cook the scallops, heat a sauté pan and add olive oil. When oil is hot, gently place the skewered scallops in the sauté pan and cook for 1 minute. Turn scallops over and cook on the other side for 1 minute. Do not overcook!

For the marinade:

1 tablespoon green tea powder

1 tablespoon sesame oil

2 cloves garlic, minced

Juice and grated zest of 2 limes

Salt and freshly ground black pepper

For the scallops:

1 pound large bay scallops

Bamboo skewers

Olive oil

For the ginger cilantro sauce:

1 cup mayonnaise

2 tablespoons honey

1 tablespoon sesame oil

1 tablespoon soy sauce

1 tablespoon minced ginger

1 tablespoon chopped cilantro

Salt and freshly ground black pepper

geronimo

executive chef | Timothy Scott

One way to experience the flavors and warmth of the Southwest is to hop on a plane and head for Santa Fe. A more convenient alternative for Nutmeggers is an evening at Geronimo. Opened in 2007, this two-level restaurant is both a tequila bar and a Southwest grill.

An adobe fireplace adds a cozy touch to the dining room where slate, walnut, and leather accents produce a handsome look. Guests can settle in at the U-shaped bar to sip a specialty or one of the one hundred types of tequila. The restaurant hosts tequila tastings to explore these varieties. "People come away learning how different [tequilas] are and that you can sip them like a good whiskey," says Elin Pistey, the restaurant's chief financial officer.

The smoky flavor of chipotle, the heat of the Sandia chile, and the designer Hatch chile lend their distinctive flavors to the Santa Fe dishes. Bison burgers, stuffed poblano chiles, and a bouillabaisse in the Santa Fe style bring a taste of the Southwest to Crown Street.

271 Crown St. | 203.777.7700
geronimobarandgrill.com

Chicken Mole with Sierra Black Beans and Poblano Rice

Chef Timothy Scott of Geronimo shares his special chicken mole recipe with us here, enticing us with a fusion of flavors. His recipe for mole sauce honors the authentic flavors of Puebla, Mexico, where it originated. The use of high-quality ingredients—three different chiles, two kinds of nuts, and Mexican chocolate—sets this mole apart from the rest.

For the red mole sauce:

6 dried guajillo chiles

6 dried ancho chiles

2 tablespoons olive oil

½ large onion, chopped

3 cloves garlic, roasted and peeled

2 large ripe tomatoes, roasted and peeled

½ cup dry roasted peanuts

¼ cup toasted sliced almonds

¼ cup toasted sesame seeds, ground to a powder

$1/16$ – ½ teaspoon espresso powder, to taste

½ teaspoon ground cumin

½ teaspoon ground coriander

½ teaspoon ground canela (Mexican cinnamon)

½ teaspoon ground allspice

2 tablespoons lard or olive oil

Salt

Chipotle chile powder, to taste

½ cup Mexican chocolate

1. Heat a skillet over medium heat; press the chiles 3 or 4 at a time onto the bottom of the pan until fragrant and pliable. Be careful not to burn them. Remove the stems and tear the softened flesh into large pieces, removing the seeds that stick to the flesh. In a small bowl, soak the chile pieces in hot water for 30 minutes, until softened.

2. Meanwhile, heat the olive oil in a small skillet over medium-high heat and sauté the onion until softened. Place the sautéed onion, roasted garlic cloves, and tomatoes in a blender and puree. Leave 1 cup of this mixture in the blender and set the rest aside. Add the peanuts, almonds, and sesame powder and blend until pureed; add a little more tomato mixture if liquid is needed. In a bowl, combine the pureed tomato mixture, peanut mixture, espresso powder, and spices.

3. Drain the chiles, reserving the soaking liquid. Place the chile pieces in the blender and add $1/4$ cup soaking liquid; use more if needed. Puree until thoroughly blended. Add the chile puree to the other purees and stir to combine thoroughly.

4. In a large saucepan heat the lard. Add the puree all at once, pouring slowly so not to splatter. Bring the mixture to a boil, reduce heat, and season with salt and chipotle chile powder. Simmer until the sauce is thick and creamy, stirring occasionally, about 20 minutes.

5. Add the chocolate and simmer for another 10 minutes. Set aside.

6. For the Sierra black beans, in a medium saucepan, heat oil until hot. Add jalapeños, garlic, and onion; sauté just until soft.

7. Add black beans and cook, stirring, for 1 minute. Add beer and simmer 5 to 8 minutes, cooking off most of the beer. Keep warm until ready to serve.

8. For the poblano rice, lightly roast poblano peppers over gas flame. When cool enough to handle, chop and set aside.

9. In a 4-quart saucepan over medium-high heat, heat the oil until hot. Add garlic and shallots and sauté until slightly softened, about 3 minutes. Add rice and stir; don't allow rice to stick to pan. Add chicken stock and poblanos, stirring once more, and bring to a boil. Lower heat to simmer, and cover the pan. Gently simmer for 15 minutes. Check rice every 5 minutes, adding water if needed. Once rice is done, add the cilantro and season with salt and pepper.

10. For the poached chicken, while the rice is cooking, begin poaching the chicken. In a large pot place the chicken stock, ancho chile powder, New Mexican red chile powder, and brown sugar. Stir until blended and bring to a light boil. Lower heat to simmer and add the chicken breasts. Simmer for 15 minutes.

11. Begin heating the mole sauce.

12. To serve, mix the sour cream and heavy cream until well blended and smooth. Set aside until ready to use.

13. Spoon rice onto a large platter or individual plates. Place chicken pieces on top of rice bed. Spoon a side of Sierra black beans on the plate next to the rice and chicken. Cover chicken with the mole sauce. Drizzle the sour cream and cream mixture over the chicken.

For the Sierra black beans:

1 tablespoon olive oil

1½ teaspoons chopped jalapeños

1 clove garlic, minced

1 tablespoon chopped onion

15 ounce can of black beans

½ bottle Sierra Nevada beer

For the poblano rice:

4 poblano peppers

1 tablespoon olive oil

1½ teaspoons minced garlic

1 tablespoon minced shallots

1 cup long-grain rice

2 cups chicken stock

2 teaspoons chopped cilantro

Salt and freshly ground black pepper

For the poached chicken:

1 quart chicken stock

2 tablespoons ancho chile powder

2 tablespoons New Mexican red chile powder

¼ cup dark brown sugar

6 boneless, skinless chicken breasts

To serve:

¼ cup sour cream

2 tablespoons heavy cream

ibiza &
ibiza tapas

executive chef | Manuel Romero

Ibiza is one of New Haven's premier restaurants, with a reputation that extends far beyond the Elm City. Its dining room is elegant and understated with interest created by well-placed splashes of color in the paintings and the curved wall of sea glass and wood that separates the bar from the dining area.

Under the direction of executive chef Manuel Romero, the upscale menu is a lively fusion of traditional and contemporary. "Our roots are in Spanish cuisine, but I like to play around with different ingredients and techniques," he says. "I use coconut milk in a sauce for diver scallops, but I also use saffron, so I don't go too far from Spanish cuisine."

On weeknights, Ibiza offers a tapas menu at the bar and a multicourse prix fixe tasting menu. At its newer Hamden outpost, the menu is strictly tapas—hot and cold little dishes and slightly larger plates—and the atmosphere is more informal.

Ibiza
39 High St. | 203.856.1993
ibizanewhaven.com

Ibiza Tapas
1832 Dixwell Ave., Hamden | 203.909.6512
ibizatapaswinebar.com

Pulpo a Feira

[Steamed Galician Octopus]

Tapas are paramount at Ibiza and pulpo a feira is offered as a small plate, warm and tasty. "Tapas" refers to a wide variety of appetizers or snacks customary in Spain. They may be eaten simply as an appetizer, but when combined they can make for a hearty meal. Cooking octopus may seem unfamiliar and adventuresome, but take a stab at this intriguing recipe—you won't be disappointed.

4 quarts water

1 medium onion, peeled and quartered

1 bay leaf

1 fresh octopus (about 3 pounds)*

Coarse sea salt

⅓ cup extra-virgin olive oil

1 teaspoon sweet paprika

1 teaspoon spicy paprika

*You can also use frozen octopus found in specialty markets and through mail order.

1. Bring water to a boil in a large stockpot, adding the onion and bay leaf.

2. While waiting for the water to boil, clean the octopus with sharp scissors: Remove and discard the ink sac, the beak between the tentacles, and the eyes; empty the head and discard contents. Wash the octopus well in cool running water. Pound the octopus heartily with a wooden mallet or rolling pin to tenderize.

3. When water is at a full boil, turn the head of the octopus inside out and, using tongs to grip, slowly dip the octopus into the water. Pull it out, wait a few seconds, and dip again; repeat for a total of 3 dips. This helps to tenderize the meat.

4. Drop the octopus into the boiling water and cook for 40 to 45 minutes.

5. Leaving the octopus in the hot water, remove the pan from the heat and set aside for about 15 minutes. Remove the octopus from the water until ready to serve.

6. Cut the octopus into large pieces and arrange on a plate. Season with salt, drizzle with the olive oil, and sprinkle with both paprikas. Serve warm.

Porrusalda

[Leek and Salt Cod Fish Soup]

Healthy, tasty, and a primary ingredient of the Mediterranean diet, seafood is key in Spanish cuisine. Bacalao, or salt cod, is one of Spain's great delights. As far back as the Romans, salting and drying were methods used to preserve fish. This soup, typical of the Basque region, becomes a hearty traditional meal when served with crusty bread, small plates of tapas, and a fabulous Spanish wine.

---

1. Submerge the salt cod in cold water and soak for at least 14 hours, changing the water two or three times. The cod will swell as it rehydrates. Drain and pat dry with paper towel. Remove the skin and bones and break the flesh into small pieces.

2. Heat the oil in a saucepan over medium-high heat. Add the garlic and sauté.

3. Add the onion, leeks, and potatoes. Stir slightly to mingle the ingredients. Cover with water and bring to a boil. Add the cod, then turn down the heat, cover, and simmer over low heat for about 40 minutes. Add salt to taste, and serve.

10 ounces dried salt cod

⅓ cup extra-virgin olive oil

4 cloves garlic, peeled and minced

½ onion, minced

4 medium leeks, washed and chopped

2 pounds potatoes, cut into medium-size chunks

Salt

We are indeed much more than what we eat, but what we eat can nevertheless help us to be much more than what we are.

—ADELLE DAVIS

john davenport's

at the Top of the Park Omni New Haven Hotel at Yale

executive chef | Jeremy Martindale

John Davenport's is a room with a view. From its perch on the nineteenth floor of the Omni hotel, the handsome dining room gives guests a different perspective on the historic city. The New Haven green, Yale's landmark buildings, and Long Island Sound lend an edge to this dining experience.

Chef Jeremy Martindale likes to cook in places with spectacular views. Before settling in New Haven, he headed up the kitchens at Little Dix Bay Resort in the British Virgin Islands, where he created award-winning cuisine, and at the Omni Interlocken Resort in Colorado, set against the backdrop of the Rocky Mountains.

Jeremy's menus celebrate the best of New England fare but with a contemporary twist. The food and service are decidedly upscale, yet choices such as braised short ribs and Georges Bank scallops are familiar and satisfying. The chef's artistic presentation of his food on stark white round or square plates is as lovely as the views.

155 Temple St. | 203.974.6859
the19thfloor.com

Crème Brûlée

Crème brûlée is French for "scorched cream" or "burnt cream," and it is a decadent dessert of rich custard topped with caramelized sugar. The custard is most often vanilla, but flavors can also include lemon, chocolate, rosemary, or any kind of fruit or liqueur. The possibilities are endless.

1 pint heavy cream

1 vanilla bean pod, split and scraped, seeds reserved

½ cup sugar

4 large egg yolks

2 quarts hot water

4 tablespoons sugar for topping

Torch for scorching

1. Preheat the oven to 325°F. Place the cream and vanilla bean pod and its seeds in a medium saucepan set over medium-high heat. Bring to a boil. Remove from heat, cover, and let sit for 15 minutes. Remove the vanilla bean pod.

2. In a medium bowl, whisk together sugar and egg yolks until well blended and just starting to lighten in color. Add the cream mixture a little at a time, stirring continually.

3. Pour the liquid into ramekins, then place ramekins into a large cake pan or roasting pan. Pour enough hot water into the pan to come halfway up the sides of the ramekins.

4. Bake just until the crème brûlée is set, but still trembling in the center, 40 to 45 minutes.

5. Remove ramekins from the roasting pan and refrigerate for at least 2 hours.

6. When ready to serve, sprinkle about 1 tablespoon sugar on top of each crème brûlée. Using a torch, melt the sugar form a crispy top. Allow the crème brûlée to sit for at least 5 minutes before serving.

Truffle Vinaigrette

MAKES ¹/₂ CUP

Truffles are the fruiting body of fungi, and they are highly prized by chefs around the world. The eighteenth-century French gastronome Brillat-Savarin called truffles "the diamond of the kitchen." This vinaigrette is delicious served over fresh greens or roasted asparagus.

1. Whisk together vinegar, truffle, salt, mustard, and pepper.

2. Add oil in a slow stream, whisking to combine.

1½ tablespoons sherry vinegar

1 bottled black truffle, finely minced

½ teaspoon kosher salt

1 teaspoon Dijon mustard

Freshly ground black pepper

4½ tablespoons canola oil or truffle oil

urban farming with focus

by ANASTATIA CURLEY

The Yale Sustainable Food Project was born in 2003 when a group of Yale students, having learned in an environmental law class about the negative effects of agricultural pesticides on human health, became determined to align Yale's everyday operations with what they were learning in their courses. These students, together with Yale president Richard C. Levin and chef and Yale parent Alice Waters, founded the Sustainable Food Project with the belief that the world's most pressing issues—from climate change and public health to the way we build community—can be positively addressed by the way we produce and share food. Today the project manages a one-acre organic garden on campus, consults on a sustainable dining program, and runs educational programs both academic and extracurricular for students and community members.

The garden, affectionately known as the Yale Farm, is at the heart of the program. Students and community members volunteer here year-round, under the guidance of a farm manager. Once a week they fire up the Yale Farm's wood-burning oven to make and share pizza topped with farm produce. Students also sell produce at CitySeed's Wooster Square farmers' market and donate a portion of the harvest to soup kitchens and community partners. The farm serves as a community space—a place to volunteer, to learn new skills, and to grow and share food.

For more information on the project, visit yale.edu/sustainablefood.

lalibela ethiopian restaurant

executive chef | Shilmat Tessema

Named after a twelfth-century church in Ethiopia, Lalibela is a prime example of the multinational restaurant scene in New Haven. For foodies looking for a different eating experience, this ten-year-old restaurant delivers.

The menu has something for everyone—shrimp, fish, chicken, beef, and lamb as well as vegetarian and vegan dishes. "The food is really healthy," says Shilmat Tessema, who took over the business two years ago. "There's not a lot of oil, and most of the dishes are light." Spices, particularly an aromatic red chile and spice blend called *berbere*, are essential to the cuisine. "It's a different kind of spice mixture," she says, "on the hot and spicy side."

The most important mealtime staple is *injera*, a spongy bread that is both eating utensil and starch. In Ethiopian culture, it's not only encouraged but proper to eat with your hands.

Lalibela ups the entertainment factor with a jazz pianist on Saturday nights, while a buffet at lunch and the option of a specialties platter at dinner allow many tastes in one meal.

176 Temple St. | 203.789.1232
lalibelarestaurantct.com

Doro Wat

[Ethiopian Chicken in Red Pepper Paste]

Doro wat is a traditional spicy Ethiopian chicken dish. The spice *berbere* is an essential ingredient, giving the dish its unique flavor. It is traditionally eaten with *injera*, a spongy flatbread made from the millet-like grain known as teff.

---

2 pounds skinless chicken legs and thighs

Juice of 1 lemon

2 teaspoons salt

¼ cup vegetable oil or melted butter

3 onions, peeled, chopped, and pureed

3 cloves garlic, peeled and crushed

1 tablespoon minced fresh ginger

¼ to ½ cup berbere paste*

¾ cup water

4 hard-cooked eggs (optional)

Injera bread for serving**

Berbere is a blend of spices and hot pepper that is mixed with water to form a paste. The spice blend is available by mail order or at Indian specialty markets. Cayenne pepper or ground chile peppers can be substituted to taste.

**To use injera traditionally, tear off a piece of the spongy bread with your hands and use it to scoop up a mouthful of the dish.*

1. Mix together the chicken pieces, lemon juice, and 1 teaspoon salt in a large, nonreactive bowl and set aside for about 30 minutes.

2. Heat the oil in a large skillet over medium-low heat and add the onions and 1 teaspoon salt. Cook for 20 to 30 minutes. Add the garlic and ginger and sauté until most of the liquid evaporates. Add the berbere paste and cook for 10 to 20 minutes, stirring frequently. Do not allow the mixture to burn.

3. Add the water and the chicken pieces. Bring mixture to a boil, reduce heat to low, cover, and simmer for 45 minutes.

4. Add the whole hard-cooked eggs, if desired, and cook for another 10 to 15 minutes or until the chicken is cooked through and very tender. Adjust seasonings to taste and serve with injera bread.

leon's

executive chef | Edward Varipapa

Edward Varipapa is well acquainted with longevity and duty to a family business. He is the fourth generation to welcome guests to Leon's, a New Haven restaurant name since 1936.

Ed's great-grandparents opened the original Leon's on the corner of Washington and Howard Streets, and his grandfather built the water-view building that houses the current Leon's on Long Wharf. The three-hundred-seat restaurant, which serves lunch, dinner, a late-night menu, and Sunday brunch, opened on New Year's Eve in 2008.

The kitchen still prepares Scampi Eugene, named for Ed's grandfather, Gypsy Chicken, and pane cotto, classic dishes that made Leon's famous. "My grandfather used to say, 'It's very easy to shine when you begin with great products,'" says Ed, who follows that advice by using fresh, seasonal ingredients and simple cooking techniques.

He honors the past but realizes that nothing stays the same. "We stay true to our roots and heritage, but I always try to present dishes as classics but plate them in a newer way." That's the way Ed brings Italian tradition to a new generation of customers.

501 Long Wharf Dr. | 203.562.5366
leonsrestaurant.com

Steak Tartare

SERVES 4

For this Leon's restaurant specialty, Ed Varipapa combines the freshest high-quality sirloin, capers, shallots, horseradish, and truffle essence, topped with Parmesan shavings and served with mâche greens.

8 ounces USDA prime sirloin, finely diced

1 tablespoon capers, diced

1 tablespoon minced shallot

1 teaspoon ketchup

½ teaspoon chopped parsley

2 teaspoons prepared horseradish

1 teaspoon soy sauce

1 teaspoon Worcestershire sauce

1 teaspoon truffle oil

¼ teaspoon freshly ground black pepper

Pecorino Romano shavings

Maldon sea salt*

Mâche lettuce

Toast points or thin crostini, for serving

Maldon salt is a flaky, delicious English sea salt.

1. In a mixing bowl, add diced sirloin, capers, shallot, ketchup, parsley, horseradish, soy sauce, Worcestershire sauce, truffle oil, and black pepper, and mix gently and thoroughly.

2. Divide seasoned sirloin among 4 chilled plates. Top with Pecorino Romano shavings, a pinch of sea salt, and lettuce. Serve with toast points or thin crostini.

Gypsy Chicken

For this classic all-around favorite at the restaurant, Ed combines semi-boneless chicken, fennel sausage, caramelized onions, hot cherry peppers, and fried potatoes with a red wine vinegar reduction.

1. Preheat the oven to 425°F. Generously season the chicken with salt and pepper.

2. Place an ovenproof sauté pan over medium heat; add the olive oil. Sauté the chicken until golden brown on one side, about 6 minutes. Turn chicken and add the sausage. Sauté both until golden brown on all sides.

3. Caramelize the Spanish onion and bake or fry the sliced potato.

4. Add the garlic to a sauté pan and, when golden brown, add the caramelized onions and potatoes. Cook for about 2 minutes.

5. Add the hot cherry peppers, oregano, wine, and vinegar and sauté for about 1 minute, until liquids reduce.

6. Add the demi-glace and finish in the oven for about 8 minutes. Lace with the extra-virgin olive oil, taste for salt and pepper, and top with parsley.

½ 2.5-pound whole chicken, deboned

Salt and freshly ground black pepper

2 tablespoons olive oil

1 Italian fennel sausage link, cut into quarters

½ Spanish onion, sliced

1 baking potato, peeled and cut into eighths

2 cloves garlic, slivered

2 vinegar hot cherry peppers, halved and seeded

¾ teaspoon chopped fresh oregano

¼ cup white wine

1 tablespoon good-quality red wine vinegar

2 tablespoons demi-glace*

1 tablespoon extra-virgin olive oil

Finely chopped flat-leaf parsley for garnish

Demi-glace can be purchased at a grocery or specialty store.

l'orcio

executive chef | Francesco d'Amuri

Francesco d'Amuri met Alison De Renzi when he was cooking at the five-star Baglioni Hotel in Florence and she was an art history student on a semester abroad program. The two fell in love, married, and traded Italy for Connecticut when they decided to establish their own restaurant.

L'Orcio, named for the decorative Tuscan urns, opened in 2003 in a pretty, two-story building, originally a home, on State Street. Francesco, a native of Puglia in southern Italy, has worked in the resort city of Rimini as well as Rome and Arezzo. His contemporary Italian menu is rooted in the wonderful regional cooking of his home-land. "We try to give people an overall Italian experience," says Alison. "This is the type of food that modern-day people in Italy eat."

Fresh, housemade pasta, including gnocchi, filled tortellini, and pappardelle, are the chef's specialties. All dishes are cooked to order and presented simply. The garnish is the aroma, Alison says.

The couple returns to Italy annually to visit family. "What we love to do most while we are there is to travel and eat," Alison says. "Our concept for L'Orcio was to share our experiences with our customers."

806 State St. | 203.777.6670
lorcio.com

Petto di Pollo
con Salsa di Finocchi

[Chicken with Fennel Sauce]

The fennel is sweetened and mellowed by slowly cooking into a puree, then topped with chicken breasts, rolled and stuffed with basil and prosciutto, for a lovely combination of flavors.

4 medium chicken breasts

Salt and freshly ground black pepper

4 paper-thin slices prosciutto di Parma

1 bunch of basil

3 tablespoons extra-virgin olive oil

1 cup white wine

1 cup chicken stock

2 bulbs fennel

1. Preheat the oven to 350°F.

2. Butterfly the chicken breasts and pound to a $1/4$-inch thickness. Lightly salt the chicken and place 1 slice prosciutto and about 5 basil leaves on each piece. Roll up each chicken breast and tie with kitchen string.

3. Place a large ovenproof sauté pan over medium-high heat; add olive oil. When oil is hot, carefully place the rolled chicken breasts into the pan and sear until golden brown. Salt and pepper to taste. Add the white wine and $1/2$ cup chicken stock. Place the pan in the oven to bake, about 15 minutes.

4. Meanwhile, wash the fennel and remove the outer parts. Cut into quarters.

5. Place fennel pieces in a small saucepan. Add $1/2$ cup chicken stock, or just enough to immerse fennel pieces. Boil until soft, about 10–15 minutes. Place the cooked fennel in a food processor and puree. Set aside.

6. When chicken is done, remove from the sauté pan (reserve pan juices) and cut each rolled breast into 3 pieces. Remove string. Set aside.

7. Add the pureed fennel to the sauté pan with the reserved pan juices. Combine and sauté until hot. Add salt and pepper to taste. If sauce is too thick, add chicken stock until desired consistency. Sauce should be smooth, creamy, and dense.

8. To serve, divide the fennel sauce among 4 dishes and place the chicken pieces on top.

Capesante Grigliate

[Grilled Scallops]

This dish is as beautiful as it is delicious. Succulent grilled scallops sitting upon a sweet red pepper puree and finished with a drizzle of green basil sauce. *Perfetto!*

1. Preheat the oven to 400°F. Place the red peppers on a cookie sheet with sides and roast in oven for about 20 minutes. Set aside to cool.

2. When peppers are cool enough to handle, peel off the skin, cut the peppers open, and remove and discard seeds and stems. Cut into strips.

3. Heat 2 tablespoons olive oil in a sauté pan over medium high heat. Sauté the pepper strips, half the chopped garlic, and salt and pepper to taste for a couple of minutes, until soft.

4. Pureé the peppers and garlic in a food processor or food mill. Set aside.

5. Clean the food processor. Reserving several whole basil leaves for garnish, add the remaining basil, 2 tablespoons olive oil, the remaining chopped garlic, and salt and pepper to taste. Process until you have a fine sauce.

6. Clean and rinse the scallops, and pat dry with paper towel. Toss the scallops in 1 teaspoon olive oil and add salt and pepper to taste. Skewer the scallops.

7. Grill scallops for $2^1/2$ minutes on each side.

8. Spoon the red pepper puree, which should be tepid, onto 4 plates.

9. Divide the scallops evenly among the plates, placing them on top of the red pepper puree. Drizzle the scallops with the basil sauce and garnish with the reserved basil leaves.

2 red bell peppers

4 tablespoons plus 1 teaspoon extra-virgin olive oil

2 cloves garlic, finely chopped

Salt and freshly ground black pepper

1 bunch of basil

Bamboo skewers

12 large diver scallops

marjolaine

executive chef | Rusty Hamilton

No Café Nervosa vibes here. The staff is welcoming, the atmosphere is laid back, and there's room to seat a baker's dozen customers at small wooden tables or on the pillowed bench. Every pastry that leaves the open kitchen, including the croissants and custom wedding cakes, is made by hand.

"We bake with love and affection and try to put a smile on everyone's face," says owner Rusty Hamilton. He took over the shop in 1986 from his mentor and Marjolaine's founder, Robert Cardinal, who trained at the Culinary Institute of America. "We make everything from scratch. It takes time—the dough has to rest and rise. Plus, we always use quality ingredients."

The shop's signature dessert is its namesake. Available by special order, the Marjolaine is a layered confection of puff pastry, hazelnut meringue, chocolate chantilly crème, and hazelnut cream topping. For more immediate enjoyment, the glass cases display a tempting collection of tea cookies, flaky palmiers, individual tarts, pastries, and cakes. Even the lowly brownie, topped with a thin layer of mocha buttercream and glazed in chocolate, gets first-class treatment here.

961 State St. | 203.789.8589
marjolainepastry.com

Swedish Chocolate Cupcakes

A Marjolaine favorite, these moist and chocolaty morsels won't last long!

2 cups plus 2 tablespoons cake flour

2 cups plus 2 tablespoons all-purpose flour

⅔ cup cocoa powder

2 teaspoons baking powder

½ teaspoon salt

1 pound butter (4 sticks), room temperature

3 cups sugar

4 eggs

2 teaspoons vanilla

1½ cups milk

1. Preheat the oven to 350°F. Line 18 standard muffin cups with paper liners.

2. In a medium bowl, sift together the cake flour, all-purpose flour, cocoa powder, baking powder, and salt. Blend well.

3. In a large bowl, cream the butter and sugar together until light and creamy. Add the eggs, one at a time, blending well between each addition. Stir the vanilla into the milk.

4. Add the dry ingredients to the egg and sugar mixture in 3 parts, alternating with the milk mixture, starting and ending with the dry ingredients.

5. Fill each muffin liner two-thirds full with the batter. Bake cupcakes until a tester comes out clean, about 20 minutes.

neighborhood noshing

by JAN ELLEN SPIEGEL

Italy rules in New Haven's small neighborhood markets that specialize in take-out food. But we're not talking any day-old Italian sub. We mean whole meals, plus catering, plus whatever momentary craving you may have. There's the Orange Street duo of Romeo & Cesare and Nica's (the two owners actually used to be partners), and Liuzzi just over the New Haven line. But there's a veritable United Nations of food as well.

Anna's
488 Orange St. | 203.782.2662
annasgourmetcatering.com

This tiny storefront is mostly home to a catering business—witness the busy kitchen in back and Mediterranean-style serving dishes stashed everywhere. But Anna Belcher serves up a healthy—and we literally mean healthy—array of take-out foods.

"I'm probably the only person in town who does brussels sprouts every day," she says. You might also find mushrooms and spinach, asparagus and potatoes, beets and carrots, chickpeas and arugula, and of course roasted mixed vegetables.

Patty and Fred Walker

Chestnut Fine Foods
1012 State St. | 203.782.6767
chestnutfinefoods.com

With an air of Provence, from the well-appointed small tables to fresh bread cooling everywhere, Chestnut is ratcheting up the take-out and catering experience. Fred (he cooks) and Patty (she bakes) Walker do original creations from scratch (with help from Patty's mom), often with local produce and cheese.

"Comfort foods fly out of here," Fred says. "We make meatloaf and mashed potatoes, and people can't get enough of them." There are fresh soups and sandwiches, a constantly changing menu of main and side dishes, and a diet-be-damned case of desserts.

Liuzzi Cheese
322 State St.
North Haven | 203.248.4356
liuzzicheese.com

Liuzzi is cheesemakers gone wild. Start with five generations of cheese-making expertise from Puglia—they make nearly twenty homemade cheeses, from mozzarella and ricotta to camorra, caciocavallo, and burrata. Then add an anything-you-can-think-of Italian deli: imported products like olive oil, tomatoes, and pasta, as well as while-you-wait sandwiches and prepared foods.

Lasagna is the biggest seller, says Domenic Liuzzi, whose father and uncle started the store. "And meatballs," he adds. "We can't keep up with them. We make sixty pounds at a time, three times a week." Not to mention the endless wheels of Parmigiano-Reggiano at "twenty, thirty wheels at a clip," Domenic says. And now they have one of the best assortments in the area of Italian, Spanish, and French cheeses.

Nica's Market
603 Orange St. | 203.787.5919
nicasmarket.com

At Nica's you can find Kraft marshmallows right next to the exotic crystallized sugars. There's pizza, a full meat market, cheeses, their own breads and pastries, a selection of local fruits and veggies in season, and some outdoor seating.

But more than anything, there's chicken—nearly two dozen chicken dishes created by owner Giuseppe Sabino (Nica is his granddaughter Veronica), some recalling his boyhood in Caserta, Italy, such as Chicken Casertana (chicken with caramelized onions) and Chicken alla Nica (with peppers and mushrooms).

"You come in, you want chicken, you have chicken. You want to have a little bit of fish, you have fish," Giuseppe (who also goes by Joe) says. "We like to make everybody happy."

Romeo & Cesare Gourmet Shoppe
771 Orange St. | 203.776.1614
romeocesare.com

What began as an Italian food import business in the 1970s has morphed into an all-purpose Italian specialty market— plus the fall 2009 addition of Romeo's Café, a few blocks south. The cafe, which serves light meals and baked goods, now provides bakery items to the store.

Choose from a half-dozen kinds of imported anchovies and tunas, local fresh produce in season, local cheeses, pizzas and stuffed breads, a salad bar, an olive bar, and a full complement of prepared dishes—mostly Italian.

"By far everybody loves our chicken cutlets," says Fran Simeone, Romeo's daughter. "I don't know what it is." Broccoli rabe, veggie lasagna, and chicken and onions are hot sellers, but, oh, those Italian combo subs.

Romeo Simeone

Westville Kosher Market
95 Amity Rd. | 203.389.1166
westvillekosher.com

Yuval and Rachel Hamenachem's grand plan was always to provide New Haven with a one-stop-shopping kosher market—meats, poultry, and a few prepared items. But over the years their prepared foods have exploded.

It's still all supervised kosher, and that includes Yuval's chicken soup, matzo balls, kugels, and stuffed cabbage, as well as Rachel's rugelach, babka, and mandelbrot.

But the most popular: "Falafel," says Yuval, who started in the food business in Israel in the 1960s. He makes his own and sells them frozen, along with his hummus and a host of Israeli and Middle Eastern foods.

mezcal

executive chef | Ricardo Trejo

Mezcal is the name of a distilled alcoholic spirit that, like tequila, is made from the agave plant. The restaurant keeps three or four kinds of its smoky-flavored namesake on hand, as well as tequilas, to make cocktails that complement the Mexican cuisine.

Ricardo Trejo, who hails from Mexico City, says he considered opening his colorful, fifty-seat restaurant in the suburbs—but only briefly. "I saw New Haven as a little New York City where ethnic food is welcome, where people are more adventurous, and where you can introduce new foods," he says.

Ricardo covered all bases, however, when he included tacos, fajitas, and chimichangas in addition to more authentic dishes on the eight-page menu. The marriage made sense: Let the more familiar plates draw in customers, who could then find "the real Mexican food."

Little by little, these traditional, regional dishes became the bestsellers at this family-friendly spot. One of the most popular recipes is straight from Ricardo's childhood: Pollo Entomatado à la Mama Gude, his mother's recipe for chicken sautéed with tomatillo, chipotle, garlic, and raisins, now outsells chimichangas.

14 Mechanic St. | 203.782.4828

Chiles Rellenos

[Stuffed Peppers]

Relleno is the Spanish word for "stuffed," and in this ethnic dish Ricardo chooses queso fresco, a soft, mild, creamy cheese. The poblano chile varies in hotness from mild to quite *picante* and is the chile of choice for this recipe.

For the peppers:

5 poblano chile peppers

1 cup all-purpose flour

3 eggs

Vegetable oil

1½ pounds queso fresco

For the sauce:

4 tomatoes, chopped

¼ Spanish onion, chopped

2 cloves garlic, minced

2 bay leaves

1 teaspoon chicken bouillon

Salt and freshly ground black pepper

Vegetable oil

1. To prepare the peppers, roast them directly on the flame of a gas stove until the skin is dark and bubbling (you can also use a griddle or a pan). Put them in a plastic bag and seal it. After a few minutes take them out and peel off as much loose skin as you can. Cut each pepper in half and remove all the seeds.

2. Place the flour on a plate. Separate the eggs, putting the whites in a large bowl. Beat the whites until they form stiff peaks, then add the yolks, mixing them well.

3. Pour about $1/2$ inch oil into a large sauté pan over medium-high heat; heat until hot.

4. Stuff the peppers with the cheese. Roll them in the flour, shaking off excess. Dip the peppers in the eggs, making sure they are completely covered with the eggs. Use tongs to carefully dip them into the hot vegetable oil. Turn them on all sides until they get brown, then put them on a plate covered with paper towels to drain off the excess oil.

5. To prepare the sauce, combine the tomatoes, onion, garlic, bay leaves, chicken bouillon, salt, and pepper with enough water to create a juicy consistency.

6. Heat the oil in a sauté pan over medium-high heat until it starts smoking. Add the sauce to the pan and sauté. Let the sauce reach a boil. Add a bit more water and let it boil until there is no more white foam, creating a lovely sauce texture.

7. Put the peppers in the pan with the sauce, and stir. Serve with rice and beans.

Tostadas de Ceviche de Camarón en Salsa Blanca

[Shrimp Ceviche Tostadas in White Sauce]

Ceviche is a citrus-marinated seafood dish adopted by many Latin American countries, each giving their individual twist to the recipe. When combined with salt, the acid in the citrus juice "cooks" the seafood, and the texture of the fish becomes firm and opaque.

1. To prepare the shrimp, put them in a bowl with enough lime juice to cover, plus a little more. Add some salt, stir lightly, and cover. Place in the refrigerator and let sit overnight.

2. To prepare the tostadas, pour oil (about 1 inch deep) into a large frying pan. Heat over high heat until oil begins to smoke. Fry the tortillas until crispy. Remove to a paper towel–lined plate. Set aside.

3. In a bowl, combine the tomatoes, onion, jalapeños, cilantro, and salt. Drain the shrimp and add to tomato mixture.

4. To prepare the sauce, mix the sour cream, mayonnaise, and lemon juice together well. Add salt, pepper, and garlic powder to taste.

5. Put a crispy corn tortilla on each plate. Spread sauce over it and top with the ceviche. Garnish with sliced avocado.

For the shrimp:

2 pounds fresh shrimp, peeled and chopped

About 1 cup freshly squeezed lime juice

Salt

For the tostadas:

Vegetable oil for frying

5 corn tortillas

4 tomatoes, finely chopped

1 medium onion, finely chopped

2 jalapeños, finely chopped

¼ cup finely chopped cilantro

Pinch of salt

Sliced avocado for garnish

For the sauce:

¾ cup sour cream

¼ cup mayonnaise

Juice of 1 lemon

Salt and freshly ground black pepper

Garlic powder

miso japanese restaurant

executive chef | Jason Tay

A wood-beam ceiling and columns as well as colorful artwork add warmth to this elegant sushi bar and restaurant in the Ninth Square district. Presiding over the sleek bamboo, brick, and stainless steel sushi bar is veteran chef Jason Tay, who has twenty-five years of experience and trained under a Japanese master. Owner Ming Lau suggests that aficionados who head for the sushi bar take advantage of Jason's specialty—a tasting menu full of surprises.

The chef and his culinary staff "can provide very authentic cuisine and fusion cuisine," Ming says. Complementing traditional tempura and teriyaki preparations are dishes such as broiled rack of lamb in Japanese plum sauce and fried soft-shell crab with guacamole and sriracha sauce.

Ingredients imported from Japan and fresh fish, inspected and chosen by Ming, arrive daily. A stickler for quality ingredients and caring service, he puts the customer first. "I tell the staff and chef that business is important but not as important as a happy customer. We truly have passion here at Miso."

15 Orange St. | 203.848.6472
misorestaurant.com

Oshitashi

[Spinach with Sesame Seed Sauce]

Sesame seed sauce is an extremely versatile dressing to have on hand. It can be made a few days ahead of time and stored in the refrigerator. Make extra and serve over hot vegetables, on a cold salad as we have here, or even as a sauce for meat.

---

2 ounces sesame seeds, toasted lightly in the oven

3 tablespoons soy sauce

3 tablespoons superfine sugar

¼ cup vegetable oil

2 tablespoons rice vinegar

1 pound spinach, washed

1. Grind the sesame seeds in a suribachi, mortar and pestle, or electric grinder.

2. Transfer the crushed seeds to a small mixing bowl and stir in soy sauce, sugar, oil, and vinegar. Mix thoroughly. The dressing will look like runny sesame butter.

3. Blanch the spinach in rapidly boiling water until the leaves are wilted, about 30 seconds.

4. Drain spinach and cool under running water for 30 seconds. Drain again and lightly squeeze out excess water.

5. Place spinach in a bowl and drizzle with sauce. Mix gently but thoroughly. Serve on individual plates or in small bowls.

Miso Sake Salmon

[Marinated Miso Salmon]

Miso is a traditional seasoning used in many Japanese dishes that is high in protein and rich in vitamins and minerals. Depending on how it is made, it can range from very salty to very sweet. It continues to gain worldwide interest.

1. Combine soy sauce, sake, mirin, miso, and sugar in a large bowl, stirring well.

2. Pat each fish steak dry with a paper towel, removing any impurities.

3. Place fish in miso sauce, cover with plastic wrap, and place in the refrigerator to marinate, about 6 hours.

4. Rinse fish and pat dry with a paper towel.

5. Grill marinated fish until desired doneness. Squeeze lemon over fish if desired.

¾ cup soy sauce

¾ cup sake

½ cup mirin (white sake)

1 pound white miso

1 cup sugar

1½ pounds 1-inch-thick salmon steaks

1 lemon, cut into wedges (optional)

You can also thread the salmon onto skewers for a different presentation.

royal palace

executive chefs | Tommy & Tony Chin

When businesses were fleeing the city for calm and a wealth of parking in the suburbs, brothers Tommy and Tony Chin did just the opposite. In 1999 they moved their popular Royal Palace restaurant from West Haven to the newly redeveloped Ninth Square district. Their fans didn't mind: "Ninety-nine percent of our customers followed us here," Tony says. "We already have the third generation of customers here."

They return for the pleasant, accommodating service and the choice of Cantonese, Mandarin, Szechuan, and Taiwanese specialties from three different menus. Tony singles out garlicky snow pea leaves, free-range chicken braised in a clay pot, tender tofu and flounder fillets, and Honey Walnut Shrimp (deep-fried shrimp tossed in mayonnaise and topped with crunchy candied nuts) as both traditional and popular dishes. The fish is so fresh, it's swimming—in a tank in a neighboring Asian grocery store where Royal Palace gets its ingredients.

Trained in Taiwan as a chef, Tommy minds the kitchen, while Tony greets guests and keeps the cheerful dining room running smoothly.

32 Orange St. | 203.776.6663
ctmenusonline.com/rp.htm

Roasted Duck

Duck meat is darker in color than that of the more popular chicken or turkey, but this makes for a stronger, richer flavor.

---

1 whole duck (4–5 pounds)

1 teaspoon five-spice powder

1 tablespoon salt

Trussing string

2–3 cups boiling water

2 tablespoons brown sugar or honey

½ tablespoon rice vinegar

2 tablespoons rice wine

1. Rinse the duck well and pat dry with a paper towel. Mix the five-spice powder and salt together. Rub the duck with the spice mixture inside the cavity. Sew up the opening with string or use toothpicks to close.

2. Tie the trussing string securely around the duck's neck or under both wings. Your goal is to hold the duck, suspended, without it slipping. Suspend the duck over the sink and pour the boiling water repeatedly over the skin until gone. This opens the pores, letting the skin absorb liquids and seasonings more easily.

3. In a bowl, mix together the brown sugar (or honey), rice vinegar, and rice wine. Spread the mixture evenly over the entire duck until well coated. Try to avoid touching the duck afterward, so as not to blemish the coating; this will result in an even coating and color. Hang the duck by the string in a well-ventilated place for about 6 hours to let it air-dry. Hanging in a cool breeze works really well to dry the skin.

4. Preheat the oven to 350°F. Place the duck in a roasting pan and roast for 45 minutes. Allow to cool for a little while, then cut into bite-size pieces. Arrange the pieces on a serving platter.

Sweet-and-Sour Spareribs

SERVES 2

There will be no leftovers here, that's for certain.

1. To prepare the ribs, rinse them in cool water and pat dry with paper towel. Cut spareribs apart, separating each rib. Carefully, cut the ribs again with a sharp knife, cutting through the bones, into $1^1/_2$-inch pieces.

2. In a bowl, mix the rice wine and soy sauce. Place the spareribs in the bowl and gently toss to coat with the marinade. Cover with plastic wrap and let sit in the refrigerator for 30 to 45 minutes.

3. Dredge the marinated ribs in the cornstarch and coat thoroughly. Set aside.

4. To prepare the sauce, combine the ketchup, sugar, rice vinegar, salt, cornstarch, and water in a bowl. Mix thoroughly and set aside.

5. Heat 3 cups oil in a wok or deep frying pan until 350°F to 375°F (drop a small piece of scallion or ginger into the oil to test; it should bubble on contact). Carefully add the spareribs to the hot oil, gently nudging to separate the ribs from one another as they cook. Let the rib pieces cook until golden brown, 3 to 4 minutes. Remove from the oil and drain on paper towels. Increase the heat of the oil to about 400°F (test with a piece of scallion; it should now sizzle noisily). Carefully add the ribs back into the oil and fry for 30 seconds, until golden and crispy. Remove and drain well.

6. In another wok or frying pan, heat 3 tablespoons vegetable oil until hot. Add the sauce ingredients. Heat until boiling. Add the spareribs and toss to coat the ribs with the sauce as they cook.

7. Remove spareribs from the wok and serve on a platter.

For the ribs:

1 pound spareribs

1 teaspoon rice wine

½ tablespoon soy sauce

1½ tablespoons cornstarch

3 cups plus 3 tablespoons vegetable oil

For the sweet-and-sour sauce:

2 tablespoons ketchup

2 tablespoons sugar

1 tablespoon rice vinegar

½ teaspoon salt

1 teaspoon cornstarch

3 tablespoons water

locally grown
in the urban landscape

by JAN ELLEN SPEIGEL

It's been a long, long time since anyone thought of New Haven as prime farming country. Indeed there are no commercial farms within the city limits anymore. But the hills and river valleys around New Haven are still dotted with them, though nowhere near to the extent they once were. The food from these farms is part of New Haven's restaurant, farmers' market, retail, and wholesale food scenes. While many chefs and others head to North Branford and farms like Northfordy, Ceccarelli, and Christofero, even closer are these in Hamden and North Haven.

Frankie's Fruit and Vegetable Stand

1940 Hartford Turnpike, North Haven | 203.376.0407

Frankie Muzio's slightly-bigger-than-a-breadbox stand sits roadside with his seven acres of farm stretching behind it. It's all the farmland left from the 158 acres his grandfather purchased in the late 1800s. But its seven acres are packed with food the way his grandfather used to grow things—nothing unnatural added.

Frankie has upwards of sixty heirloom tomato varieties, plus every vegetable you can think of, plus white corn, peaches, a range of berries, and chickens (for eggs only). And none of this picked-the-night-before stuff: Frankie picks everything the same day or even better. "You come to my store and say 'Frankie, I want a romaine,' and I go out and cut it," he says. "You get food the way it's supposed to taste. I cater to you, the customer."

Frankie's is open May 1 until October 31, except for the eggs—just call a day ahead and they'll be waiting for you.

Hindinger Farm

835 Dunbar Hill Rd., Hamden | 203.288.0700
hindingersfarm.com

You can't find much more local heritage than at Hindinger Farm. Started in 1893, it is now run by fourth-generation Hindingers—the brother and sister team of George and Liz Hindinger.

They farm about one hundred acres of their 138 total—a stunning south-facing spread with a view of New Haven and Long Island Sound. About fifty acres are covered with fruit trees. The biggest crop after that is sweet corn, followed by everything from asparagus to zucchini. Most everything is sold at their farm store, along with other local products, spring through Christmas. You can also find their produce at a few area farmers' markets as well as anonymously in the wholesale and restaurant food chain.

But really, George and Liz kind of chuckle when they talk about local food. "Wouldn't we be the originator since we've been serving up local food for so long?" Liz asks. "People's conception is we're so far away, but we're really not. We're a few minutes away from Dixwell Avenue."

"We don't want local food to be a trend," George says. "We want it to be a habit."

Mill River Valley Gardens
3600 Ridge Rd., North Haven | 203.248.2096

Hidden in the rolling North Haven hills, Walter Greist's farm is more of an overgrown garden—only about two acres. But these have been seminal acres in Connecticut agricultural history. In 1989, Walter's farm became the first community supported agriculture (C.S.A.) operation in the state. People buy shares in exchange for weekly food allotments—and he hopes they'll help on the farm, too.

"I think it's important for people to see that they're part of an ecosystem, and this gives them an opportunity to be producers as well as consumers," explains Walter, who plans to transfer farm ownership to his C.S.A. members.

In the meantime, the only way to get Walter's summer produce and his specialty, Asian greens, is to join the C.S.A. "You can do without most manufactured products," he says. "But you can't do without food."

Two Guys From Woodbridge
4066 Whitney Ave., Hamden | 203.281.5559

Really just one guy from Hamden—Perry Hack—who since 2003 has been using hydroponics to push greens to a year-round level never seen in New Haven, or Connecticut, for that matter. His blemish-free rows of everything from arugula to shungiku and a whole bunch of other stuff you have and haven't heard of are in greenhouses. They grow in crushed coconut shells in troughlike contraptions called channels infused with perfectly attenuated water and nutrients.

It makes him one of the only year-round greens operations in the state, and you can find his products—including microgreens and edible flowers—at farmers' markets, specialty markets, and restaurants in the region. Most items are sold with the roots still attached, so they last longer and, truth be told, they're so pretty you could use them as centerpieces instead of food.

It's an expensive way to do business, though, and that means pricier produce. But the way Perry sees it, "People are getting a superior product and things that are a lot fresher." You can't argue with that.

Manager Jeff Horton and Jeff Caputo

scoozzi

executive chef | Jeff Caputo

Even after twenty-plus years in downtown New Haven, Scoozzi knows how to keep things fresh and lively. The menu, rooted in Italian cuisine, must constantly evolve and change, says executive chef Jeff Caputo. For inspiration, Jeff looks to the motherland and the trattorias that prize fresh ingredients so highly.

Going beyond Connecticut-grown produce, he has added local meats, cheeses, and wines to his pantry. A blend of locally produced natural ground beef and sausage becomes Scoozzi's lunch burger, while the dinner scallops are harvested off Stonington and garnished with local vegetables and honey. "We're trying to use local, what's available and indigenous," he says. "We've created our own little Italian cuisine, based on the spirit of the Italian trattoria."

Sunday brunch draws customers not only for the a la carte offerings but also for the entertainment of jazz guitarist Tony Lombardozzi.

Just steps away from Yale Repertory Theater and art museums, Scoozzi has the three L's of real estate sewn up. In warm-weather months, the garden patio—a country oasis in an urban setting—offers as charming a backdrop for good food and drink as the colorful dining room.

1104 Chapel St. | 203.776.8268
scoozzi.com

Insalata Arugula

[Arugula Salad]

This salad is one of Jeff's favorites. Arugula is often peppery and smoky in its range of flavors, which vary depending on the crop. It blends well with an acid-based dressing and if only one dressing was chosen for it, it would be the honey-lemon. The dressing unites with the boldness of the green in a perfect marriage. When you add in the red onion, Gorgonzola, and the rest, the balance is delightful. It is refreshing and invigorating. Food at its best should be enjoyed with minimal ingredients, each speaking for itself within the harmony of the dish. The result: a minimal-effort masterpiece.

Juice of 3 lemons

1 tablespoon honey

9 ounces baby arugula, washed and dried

1 small red onion, sliced as thin as possible

3 ounces Lombardian Gorgonzola (or your choice) cheese, crumbled

36 seedless red grapes, washed and dried

1 orange, skin and seeds removed, diced into bite-size pieces

1 ounce pignoli (pine nuts), toasted lightly in the oven

1. Combine the lemon juice and honey in a medium bowl, and whisk together until smooth.

2. Add the remaining ingredients to the bowl and toss lightly with your hands. Don't press on the greens; treat them gently so as to not bruise them or the other ingredients. Thoroughly incorporate all the dressing with the ingredients (which should take less than a minute).

> Italian cuisine has no boundaries;
> it is a cuisine based on availability.
> So why not take advantage of it and
> create a new dish of your own?
>
> —JEFF CAPUTO

Pappardelle d'Estate

[Summer Pappardelle]

Jeff Caputo chose to share this entree because of its popularity and versatility. It is simplicity at its best and can also be easily altered to allow for dietary restrictions by omitting the heavy cream and butter and simply tossing it in excellent-quality extra-virgin olive oil. Also, these ingredients are readily available most of the summer.

1. Preheat the oven to 350°F. Place the corn on a baking sheet with sides and roast 10 minutes. Remove from oven and let it stand until cool enough to handle. Place a cob in a bowl and, with a sharp knife, cut the kernels from the cob, letting them fall into the bowl.

2. Set a pot of water over high heat to boil, for the pasta.

3. Meanwhile, heat the oil in large sauté pan (or medium sauce pot) to fairly high heat. Add corn, asparagus, tomatoes, and mushrooms. Sauté them for 2 minutes, then add the wine, being careful of flare-ups. Let it reduce a bit, then add the cream. Lower the heat to a steady simmer. Let the mixture reduce until it reaches sauce consistency (so it coats a spoon but isn't too wet). If it's too thick, add a couple of ounces of the pasta water after you cook the pasta in it. Add the butter, salt, and pepper. Remove from heat.

4. Add some salt and the pasta to the boiling water and cook until al dente, about 8 minutes. Drain the pasta, reserving some water if necessary, and immediately add it to the sauce. Grate some Pecorino Romano cheese over the top, toss lightly, and serve.

3 ears corn, husked

¼ cup olive oil

1 bunch asparagus, cut into ¾-inch segments, tough root ends discarded

2 ounces sundried tomatoes, cut into ¼-inch strips

1 pound sliced mushrooms (buttons and creminis mixed)

1 cup Marsala wine

1¼ cups heavy cream

2 tablespoons butter

Salt and freshly ground white pepper

1 package pappardelle (Scoozzi prefers De Cecco brand)

Pecorino Romano cheese

skappo
italian wine bar

executive chef | Anna & Marc Gambacorta

Dining at Skappo is a family affair. Mama Anna Gambacorta's domain is the kitchen where, with son Marc at her side, she prepares the Umbrian dishes of her childhood. Anna's husband, architect Thomas Sincavage, designed the cozy sliver of a restaurant and Skappo Merkato, their Italian specialty food shop around the corner. Their son Michael chooses the wines, while his sister Yvette makes the breads and desserts. In the evening, the pair keep the dining room humming.

Anna, an energetic and personable slip of a woman, pops out of the kitchen to greet her guests and make sure everyone is happy. Her menu is a mix of traditional dishes, family recipes, and new creations in the Assisi style. The menu suggests wine pairings from the lengthy list of red, white, sparkling, and dessert wines from all regions of Italy.

Often on Tuesday evenings music turns up on the menu. Marc leaves the kitchen to front his band in the dining room, while guests enjoy a prix fixe pasta dinner to the tunes of the band's favorite pop artists.

59 Crown St. | 203.773.1394
skappo.com

Torta al Testo

Torta al testo is a very traditional flatbread that is found within the central region of Italy, called Umbria. It is such a staple in the Umbrian diet that there is even a specific pan that was created for baking this bread, though a cookie sheet works just as well. The delicate torta can be sliced in half and filled with various grilled vegetables, sautéed greens, tangy cheeses, and an assortment of meats or used as a base for numerous toppings and home-made spreads. This recipe uses the torta in just that manner, as a base for a delicious combination of thinly sliced meat and a traditional Umbrian cheese.

3 cups all-purpose flour

½ teaspoon salt

½ teaspoon freshly ground black pepper

1 tablespoon sugar

⅔ cup grated Parmesan cheese

2 tablespoons fennel seeds

1 tablespoon baking powder

⅓ cup vegetable shortening

1 cup warm milk

1 tablespoon water

1 tablespoon olive oil

1. Preheat the oven to 375°F. Combine all the dry ingredients and the vegetable shortening in a large bowl. Slowly add the warm milk to the mixture, stirring. Work the mixture until a soft dough forms. Knead it for 5 minutes. Roll the dough into a rectangular form and lay it on a cookie sheet.

2. Combine the water and oil and lightly sprinkle the dough with oil mixture. Bake until golden brown, 15 to 20 minutes.

3. Place the pan on a rack to cool. Cut the torta into rectangular slices of desired size.

Crostino Umbro

1. Preheat the oven to 375°F. Melt the butter in a small saucepan over medium-high heat. Add the flour, stirring vigorously to combine the ingredients and avoid clumping. When the butter and flour mixture is smooth, stir in the warm milk. Stir constantly until the mixture thickens to a creamy texture, 5 to 8 minutes.

2. Remove from heat and add the grated Parmesan cheese; add salt and pepper to taste.

3. Place the torta slices on a baking sheet and spread a thin layer of white sauce on each slice; place 2 slices prosciutto cotto and then 2 thin shavings Pecorino di Fossa on top.

4. Bake the crostini in the oven until the cheese is light golden brown and slightly melted, about 15 minutes.

2 tablespoons butter

¾ cup all-purpose flour

1½ cups warm milk

¼ cup grated Parmesan cheese

Salt and freshly ground black pepper

8 pieces of torta al testo (recipe on facing page)

16 slices prosciutto cotto*

16 very thinly shaved slices Pecorino di Fossa**

*A delicately sweet baked ham that can be found at Skappo Merkato or any high-end specialty meat store.

**A specialty Umbrian sheep's milk cheese that has been aged in a cave for one hundred days.

soul de cuba

executive chefs | Robert & Jesus Puerto

Cuban food remains a novelty in Connecticut, where restaurants specializing in the ethnic cuisines of Italy, China, and Japan are more numerous. Jesus and Robert Puerto, brothers whose grandfather was a Cuban immigrant, have been treating adventurous restaurant-goers to their brand of Cuban and African food since 1995.

Some dishes are traditional; others treat ingredients in a more contemporary way. The signature Pollo Soul de Cuba is an example of updated cooking. A marinated, breaded, and fried chicken breast with Chef Robert's salsa of mango, guava, black beans, pineapple, and rum has become the lengthy menu's bestseller. Foodies who want to "bring the flavor home"—the chef's slogan for his bottled sauces, marinades, and salsa—can buy his products at the restaurant.

Cuban salsa music or African or American jazz plays quietly in the background, and family photographs and colorful Afro-Cuban artwork decorate the coffee-colored walls. Yale students and professors are regular customers, says manager Matthew Bedard, who spent two years working at the sister Soul de Cuba in Honolulu. Despite the distance, Bedard sees similarities between the customers at both restaurants: "They are all open to trying new things."

83 Crown St. | 203.498.2822
souldecuba.com

Picadillo

Picadillo is a traditional dish in many Latin American countries and the Philippines. While ingredients vary by region, it is most often served with rice or as a filling. "Picadillo" comes from the Spanish *picar*, which means to mince or chop.

3 tablespoons olive oil

2½ pounds ground beef

1¼ teaspoons minced garlic

¼ teaspoon Goya-brand adobo

⅓ cup white vinegar

½ onion, finely chopped

½ red bell pepper, finely chopped

½ green bell pepper, finely chopped

1 packet Goya-brand sazón achiote

⅓ cup sliced Spanish olives

½ cup capers

½ cup tomato sauce

Rice for serving

Parsley for garnish

1. Heat the olive oil in a frying pan over low heat. Add ground beef, garlic, adobo, and vinegar. Sauté, breaking the ground beef into small pieces, until beef is uniformly a light brown color.

2. Strain out most of the fat, and add onion, peppers, sazón, olives, capers, and tomato sauce. Cover and simmer for 20 minutes.

3. Serve picadillo over rice on a large serving platter or divide among individual plates. Garnish with a spring of parsley.

Sopa de Garbanzo

SERVES 4–6

Otherwise known as chickpea soup, sopa de garbanzo is a hearty and healthy soup. It's also a one-pot meal, which makes it easy and convenient.

1. Drain and rinse the garbanzo beans in a colander.

2. Using one of the empty bean cans, measure 5 cans water into a large soup pot. Add the garbanzo beans and remaining ingredients to the soup pot and simmer until flavors are combined and soup is aromatic, about 30 minutes.

5 15.5-ounce cans garbanzo beans

½ medium Spanish onion, diced

½ medium green bell pepper, diced

1 chorizo sausage, cut into 1-inch slices

3 cloves garlic

½ tablespoon allspice

½ teaspoon freshly ground black pepper

3 teaspoons salt, or to taste

1 teaspoon chicken bouillon

pie city

by LINDA GIUCA

There is one food in New Haven that inspires fierce loyalty, prompts heated arguments, and compels people to queue up in summer's humidity or winter's frigid air for the opportunity to savor it.

Pizza. A slice made up of elementary ingredients—crust, tomato, cheese—has earned New Haven a treasured spot on America's gastronomic map. If there is a chance of a better pie, the pizza aficionado must hop a plane to Naples, where the phenomenon began.

Otherwise, a trip to one of New Haven's legendary pizzerias is all it takes to experience the best pies this side of the Atlantic. No one agrees on who makes the best pizza in town, but a few names pop up in every discussion.

Pepe's, officially Frank Pepe Pizzeria Napoletan, estab-lished in 1925 on Wooster Street, is the granddaddy of the city's pizza parlors. Its competition, Sally's Apizza, opened in 1938, just down the block, on the north end of the street. Modern Apizza chose a different neighborhood when its reign began on State Street in 1934.

Modern also set itself apart from its Wooster Street competition by offering grinders, calzones, and entrees in addition to the specialty of the house. At Sally's and Pepe's, the menu is pizza, pizza, and more pizza.

The old-timers sometimes compete with upstarts who may not have decades of experience behind them but turn out great pies that earn raves in restaurant junkies' forums. When the dance spot and nightclub Bar opened in 1991 in an old car showroom on Crown Street, its distinctive design won an award from the Connecticut Institute of Architects. In 1996, the owners earned a different kind of accolade with the addition of the Bru Room, a destination for brick-oven pizza and microbrewed beer. Regulars swear by the cracker-thin crusts and urge newbies not to miss the pie with the fluffy mashed potato topping.

In these famous pizzerias, the thin-crusted beauties emanate from coal- or wood-fired ovens that create the obligatory slightly charred bottom and turn bread dough into a crisp yet slightly chewy wonder. The epitome of New Haven–style pizza is really a "less is more" pie—crust, tomato sauce, a sprinkle of grated cheese, and, maybe, a touch of oregano or garlic.

Even the city's signature pie is quite simple—that fabulous crust topped with briny fresh-shucked clams, garlic, olive oil, and grated Parmesan. It has inspired rhapsodic prose from food critics and bitter disappointment when fresh clams aren't available.

At busy times, waiting in line for admittance to the more popular pizzerias can turn the most mild-manned restaurant-goer into a cranky killjoy. But once inside the inner sanctum, all is forgiven. The energy feels rejuvenating. Watching the pizzamakers stretch and toss the dough, wield the peel, and lift those bubbling hot pies from the floor of the brick oven becomes the first course of the meal. The mouth waters as the anticipation builds. When that free-form round pie arrives at the table, nothing else matters.

Food trends will come and go. Memorable meals will take place in restaurants with far more star power than a pizza parlor. But there is something real and universally pleasing about pizza, and, when that craving takes hold, New Haven has the best to offer.

Frank Pepe Pizzeria Napoletana
157 Wooster St. | 203.865.5762
pepespizzeria.com

Sally's Apizza
237 Wooster St. | 203.624.5271
sallysapizza.net

Modern Apizza
874 State St. | 203.776.5306
modernapizza.com

Bar
254 Crown St. | 203.495.8924
barnightclub.com

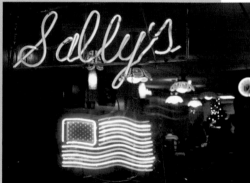

temple grill

executive chef | Tony Marchitto

Temple Grill, which opened in 2004, has a great vibe. It's simple—hardwood floors, exposed brick walls, and lots of windows—casual, and at times noisy, yet the hum of conversation only adds to the friendly atmosphere. It's the kind of urban neighborhood spot that draws apartment dwellers a few times a week for an old-fashioned supper of Yankee pot roast or grilled meatloaf.

Chef and co-owner Tony Marchitto, who trained at the Culinary Institute of America in Hyde Park, New York, calls his food "rustic American regional cuisine." The food is honest, the choices are numerous, and Marchitto takes the idea of "give the customers what they want" to a new level. A salad card allows guests to check off the ingredients they want—the kind of greens, mix-ins, proteins, dressing, and toppings. The same concept extends to the menu's create-your-own pasta category. Another nice touch is that entrees and pastas are available as either full or half portions.

Marchitto has found success with straightforward food. Capture the natural flavors of good ingredients, he believes, and let the customers really enjoy what they're eating.

152 Temple St. | 203.773.1111
templegrill.com

Sautéed Tenderloin Tips with Lobster Bourbon Cream Sauce

Along with the famous design-your-own salads and mouthwatering entrees, this succulent dish is one of Temple Grill's bestsellers. It is a classic favorite and was actually the Temple Grill's original recipe. As Tony says, "It was the first dish I created when designing the concept for the restaurant's food style and menu. It set the tone for the restaurant."

---

1 8-ounce beef tenderloin, trimmed

2 tablespoons butter

1 shallot, minced

2 scallions, sliced thin

½ cup bourbon

½ cup heavy cream

¼ cup demi-glace*

Salt and freshly ground black pepper

4 ounces cooked lobster meat, picked over for shells

2–4 asparagus spears, steamed

You can purchase professional-quality demi-glace, ready-made.

1. Cut the tenderloin into 1-inch cubes.

2. Melt the butter in a sauté pan over medium-high heat. Add the tenderloin pieces. Sear the meat evenly, stirring gently.

3. Add shallot and scallions; cook over medium-high heat until meat is half done, 6 to 8 minutes, turning the meat midway through. The meat should be medium rare.

4. Add bourbon and cook to reduce liquid by three-quarters. Add cream and reduce until it starts to thicken.

5. Add demi-glace and salt and pepper to taste.

6. Finally, add the lobster to the sauce and stir gently.

7. To plate, center the tenderloin on a plate. Using a large spoon, dish a helping of sauce over the meat. Top with a cross-cross of 2 to 4 asparagus spears.

teaching good food

by VALERIE BANNISTER

Since 2008, Tim Cipriano has been the executive director of food services for the New Haven public schools. He has been working to provide the city's students with fresh, healthy, local foods—sixteen thousand lunches are served every day—as well as teaching students how to make healthy food choices for themselves and the planet.

As of this writing, Chef Tim, as he is known, was taking his mission one step further, looking for farmland for educational purposes and for agricultural production, modeled after a program in Baltimore called the Great Kids Farm of the Baltimore City Public Schools.

Chef Tim has more than sixteen years of experience in culinary arts, both in schools and restaurants, and is involved in a variety of organizations promoting local food, such as the state's Farm-to-Chef program and Farm-to-School program.

Also known as the Local Food Dude (he created a Web site that bears that name), Chef Tim has received local and national recognition for his efforts in promoting local food, including a Connecticut Climate Change Award from Connecticut governor Jodi Rell and the Connecticut Department of Environmental Protection.

Chef Tim's Web site, which states that it's "devoted to increasing the consumption of locally grown foods," offers this recipe for Squapple Crisp, which includes winter squash and apples and was created when Chef Tim was working with students at Dodd Middle School in Cheshire.

squapple crisp

4 cups peeled, seeded, and diced winter squash

½ stick (4 tablespoons) butter

½ cup maple syrup

⅛ teaspoon nutmeg

¼ teaspoon cinnamon

1 cup Nature's Path Flax Plus Flakes, crushed

1 pound (about 3) apples, peeled and sliced

1. Preheat the oven to 350°F. Place squash cubes on a rimmed cookie sheet and roast squash until tender.

2. Mash the squash with 1 tablespoon butter, 1/4 cup maple syrup, and the spices.

3. In a saucepan, melt the remaining 3 tablespoons butter. Mix with the flax cereal and remaining syrup.

4. Layer squash and apple slices in a baking pan, then top with flax mixture. Bake until bubbling, 15 to 20 minutes. Serve hot alone as a side dish or with a scoop of vanilla ice cream.

the terrace

executive chef | Amy Wongwiwat

"I am the waiter, and she is the chef," says Jeff Wongwiwat, who proudly explains his wife Amy's cooking philosophy and the bones of each dish. In Amy's capable hands, her food achieves the balance of spicy, sour, sweet, and salty that is an essential element of Thai cuisine.

"Our theme is to really cook very authentic Thai food, but sometimes, when we can, we add a French presentation," Jeff says. The melding of the two cuisines reflects Amy's background. Born in Bangkok, she learned to cook when she was eight years old. As an adult, she lived in France, where she trained for a year with legendary French chef Paul Bocuse.

The spanking white building and the minimalist decor are as clean and fresh as the flavors of the Thai cuisine served in this tiny restaurant. The menu is extensive, and the wine and beer list is well chosen to complement the meal. Personable and welcoming, the Wongwiwats opened the Terrace in 2007. They chose Hamden rather than downtown New Haven because they wanted to "give back" to the town where they also live.

1559 Dixwell Ave., Hamden | 203.230.2077
theterracethai.com

Green Curry Shrimp

Green curry is a variety of curry used in Thai cuisine. Curry dishes are often named for their color. There are red and yellow curry dishes as well. Red curries are spicy, as are green curry dishes, though the green curry offers a certain sweetness that other curry dishes lack.

2 tablespoons vegetable oil

2 tablespoons green curry paste

1½ cups coconut milk

2 tablespoons sugar

1 tablespoon fish sauce

12 fresh peeled shrimp (medium or large)

1½ ounces green beans, trimmed

1 red bell pepper, diced

1 green bell pepper, diced

2 ounces bamboo shoots, sliced

¼ cup water

15 fresh Thai basil leaves

Salt

1. Heat the oil in a medium pot over low heat. Add green curry paste and sauté until the smell of the paste rises up. Add the coconut milk, sugar, and fish sauce. Stir together and heat to a boil over medium heat.

2. Add the shrimp and cook, watching carefully for them to turn pink (be careful to not overcook). Add green beans, bell peppers, and bamboo shoots. Add water and bring to a boil, stirring.

3. Add basil leaves and remove curry from heat. Add more sugar or salt if desired.

Green curry can be cooked with chicken, beef, pork, tofu, vegetables, or seafood. Chef Amy personally favors it with Thai spaghetti.

A variety of fresh greens grown in the hydroponic greenhouses at Two Guys from Woodbridge, in Hamden

thali &
thali too

executive chef | Prasad Chirnomula

Prasad Chirnomula's father pushed for his son to become a doctor. Lucky for the food world, Prasad chose culinary school over medical college. Reviewers sing his praises, going as far as dubbing him the "most exciting Indian chef in the United States." Prasad's way with spices and his contemporary approach to regional Indian dishes are both educational and delicious. Dishes such as Konkan Crab seasoned with ginger, mustard seeds, coconut, and green chiles and Thali's signature lamb chops, marinated in spices and yogurt, are served in a dining room that is at once sleek, elegant, and exotic.

Prasad caters to a frugal, vegetable-loving crowd at Thali Too, where meat is taboo and prices stay under $10. In the lassi bar, frothy yogurt drinks, both plain and spiked, are the signature "cocktails," while the make-your-own rice bar lets guests be creative. In warm weather, guests can people-watch on the patio under the shade of the large red market umbrellas.

Thali
4 Orange St. | 203.777.1177
thali.com

Thali Too
65 Broadway | 203.776.1600
thalitoo.com

Hyderabadi Biryani with Lamb

If there is a jewel in the crown of Hyderabadi cooking, this is it. The Moghuls brought their lovely mild, buttery, Persian-influenced biryani down from the north and Hyderabadi chefs turned it into a flavor volcano. All over India, when foodies think of Hyderabad, they think of biryani first, despite the dish's northern roots. It's great for a grand dinner party dish because you can make it earlier in the day, set it aside in its covered pot, then at the table, serve the warm, fragrant, richly flavored rice and lamb to your swooning guests.

For the meat:

2 teaspoons pureed green papaya*

2 cups plain yogurt

2 tablespoons ginger-garlic paste (see recipe)

2 tablespoons red chili powder

1 tablespoon lemon juice

1 tablespoon garam masala

1 tablespoon coriander

1 tablespoon salt

1 teaspoon turmeric

¼ teaspoon ground nutmeg

2 cups firmly packed fried onions (see recipe)

¼ cup firmly packed chopped fresh mint leaves

¼ cup firmly packed chopped fresh cilantro leaves

1 heaping tablespoon julienned fresh ginger

4 small green chiles, cut into thin slivers

2 pounds lamb, with bone, cut into 1½-inch cubes

1. To prepare the meat, in a large pot with a tight-fitting lid, mix papaya puree, yogurt, ginger-garlic paste, red chili powder, lemon juice, garam masala, coriander, salt, turmeric, nutmeg, 1 cup fried onions, mint, cilantro, ginger, and green chiles. Mix well and add the lamb so that it is submerged. Cover with a tight-fitting lid or dough (see sidebar) and let meat marinate for 2¹/₂ hours at room temperature.

2. Meanwhile, to prepare the rice, place rice in a bowl and add enough water to cover. Using your hands and fingertips, scrub the rice for a minute or two. Drain off the water and let rice sit in the bowl for 2¹/₂ hours.

3. Place saffron threads, 1 teaspoon salt, and ¹/₂ cup warm water in a small bowl and let soak for 1 hour at room temperature.

4. When rice has soaked, bring 6 cups water to a boil. Add 1 teaspoon salt, the chiles, bay leaves, cinnamon, black peppercorns, cloves, cardamom seeds, cumin seeds, and oil to the water and let boil for 3 minutes. Drain the rice and add it to the pot; let it return to a boil. Boil for exactly 3 minutes. Use a slotted spoon to lift the rice from the pot, picking up the flavoring spices as well. Spoon half the rice and spices over the marinated meat. (It's okay if some of the rice cooking liquid makes its way to the meat pot.) Add the remaining cup of fried onions. Finish by topping the pot with the remaining rice and spices.

An authentic twist on this recipe would be to seal the pot with a dough paste. The paste is made of all-purpose flour and water mixed to form a stiff dough. It is then formed into a snake that fits around the circumference of the pot. The lid is set firmly in place on the dough to form the seal.

—PRASAD CHIRNOMULA

Ginger-Garlic Paste

½ cup peeled fresh ginger chunks

½ cup whole peeled garlic cloves

1 tablespoon vegetable oil

Place the ginger, garlic, and oil, plus a few drops of water, in a food processor and puree to a smooth paste.

5. Evenly drizzle $^1/_3$ cup ghee over meat and rice. Then carefully drizzle the saffron water as evenly as possible over the rice. Cover the pot with a tight-fitting lid.

6. Place the pot on high heat and cook for 12 minutes. Turn down the heat to very low and simmer for another 40 minutes.

7. Remove the pot from heat and allow to sit for 30 minutes. The dish can then be held for 5 to 6 hours, at room temperature, before serving.

Fried Onions

MAKES 2 CUPS

2 large Spanish onions, peeled and sliced into thin rings

1 cup vegetable oil

Pour oil into a large pot and place over medium-high heat. Heat the oil to 325°F. Drop the onion rings into the oil and cook until they are a dark, golden brown, 5 to 7 minutes.

Remove the onions and drain on paper towels. Reserve at room temperature for use that day, or refrigerate for future use.

For the rice:

2 cups basmati rice

½ teaspoon saffron threads

2 teaspoons salt

6½ cups water

2 green chiles

2 bay leaves

2 cinnamon sticks

20 black peppercorns

6 cloves

12 whole green cardamom seeds

2 whole black cardamom seeds

½ teaspoon black cumin seeds

⅓ cup vegetable oil

⅓ cup ghee (clarified butter)**

* Green papaya may be difficult to find. Check a well-stocked greenmarket. Buy it when you see it and puree and freeze it for future use. Since the purpose of the papaya is to tenderize the meat, you can substitute a little store-bought tenderizer at the same stage of preparation.

**Ghee is a clarified butter without any solid milk particles or water. It is a staple in Indian cooking.

Konkan Crab

A signature appetizer from Thali, this recipe is an easy one to make at home. The ginger, mustard, green chile, and coconut blend to make a unique, flavorful dish that you'll want to make again and again.

2 tablespoons butter

¼ teaspoon black mustard seeds

2 cloves garlic, chopped

½ teaspoon peeled and chopped ginger

8 curry leaves

1 serrano chile (or your favorite chile), chopped

1 medium-size red onion, peeled and finely chopped

1 pound jumbo lump crab

Salt and freshly ground black pepper

1 cup coconut milk

Juice of ½ lemon

1. Heat a heavy-bottomed sauté pan over high heat to smoking point. Reduce heat to medium, and add butter. After 30 seconds, add mustard seeds, garlic, ginger, curry leaves, chile, and onion. Stir for 2 minutes and increase heat to high. Add crab, salt, and pepper. Cook for 1 minute. Add coconut milk, and cook for 5 minutes, until reduced, scraping sides and bottom of pan.

2. Mix in the lemon juice, and serve hot over rice.

I love the food of this exotic south-central Indian city. Hyderabad's uniqueness was assured centuries ago, when the Muslim rulers of the north lost their power base and fled south. Hyderabad, already steeped in southern cooking tradition, was the place where they established a new empire. The northern Moghuls brought with them the best of northern cooks.

—PRASAD CHIRNOMULA

cultivating lives

by VALERIE BANNISTER

Common Ground is firmly rooted in the New Haven environment and local food movement. Yet it is also a place set apart.

It is a charter high school, organic farm, and nonprofit environmental education center, located on twenty acres at the base of West Rock Ridge State Park at the edge of the city. And it is that particular site—"a school, on a farm, in a state park, in a city"—that makes it special, says Joel Tolman, director of development and community engagement.

The seed of the organization started in the 1980s with a group of parents and teachers who wanted to teach environmental education and connect youth to natural resources in New Haven. In the 1990s, the group evolved into the nonprofit New Haven Ecology Project, and in 1997 Common Ground High School, an environmental and college preparatory school, became one of the first charter schools in Connecticut.

Today the mission of Common Ground—including farm, nature center, and high school—is to "cultivate habits of healthy living and sustainable practice among a diverse group of children, families, and adults," says Tolman.

It is through one or all of those doors that people enter Common Ground. The farm sells produce at a farmers' market in Edgewood Park (not far away); the nature center invites schools and community members to Common Ground for field trips, summer camps, and family programs; and the high school enrolls 150 students, who get free public transportation to school and lunches prepared with food from the organic garden.

High school students might participate in an Environmental Ventures class, in which they create their own products with farm produce—such as salsa—or a class in which they take care of the site, doing farm work and emptying the cafeteria's compost bin.

All the components of Common Ground—farm, nature center, and school—are interrelated. Its location—in a state park and a city—allows students and the community to explore the usually not-so-visible relationship between farm, forest, and city.

As a result of Common Ground, opportunities to take

a guided walk in the woods, look eye-to-eye with a turkey, or pick some parsley right out of the garden are available a stone's throw from the city.

By the same token, students can investigate the urban environment, as well as take advantage of its rich resources. The school is working with the Yale Peabody Museum of Natural History to create an interpretive outdoor walk and is working with the Yale Urban Resources Initiative to plant trees in the city and study their impact.

After maneuvering through traffic, noise, and lights, the first obvious sign that one is near the school is West Rock Ridge State Park's seven-mile-long red cliff rising more than six hundred feet, towering over homes on the city's outskirts. Homes give way to forest and stream, and, turning into the school's driveway, it seems as if one has come upon a small farm in Vermont.

There are homemade signs, a large "working" garden, a smaller "educational" garden, mulch heaps, and two educational buildings, one on the site of an old farmhouse. There are pens of chickens, turkeys, ducks, goats, and sheep; plastic-covered greenhouses (larger ones are planned to extend the growing season); picnic tables; and signs for trails leading the way into the forest and to the top of the steep cliff.

Walking around the smaller garden, Tolman says, "It's a really valuable lesson in where food comes from." He said most of what's grown there, such as sorrel, can be picked and eaten right away. "It's a shocking, exciting taste that will stick with them [visitors] when they leave," he says.

The larger, "working" garden provides some five thousand pounds of produce annually , about half of which helps feed the students, while the rest goes to the farmers' market.

Rebecca Holcombe, director of community programs, says, "I love connecting folks in the city to nature and food." She says Common Ground runs a popular seedling sale and a pancake breakfast at which people learn about tapping trees for sap and making maple syrup.

On one fall walk in the 1,800-acre park, she took about twenty people from the farm through the forest to the top of the cliff (part of a series of ridges extending to Vermont and formed two hundred million years ago), providing a bird's-eye view of the entire landscape. She told hikers, who could see all the way to New Haven Harbor, "It's really fun to come up here and see where you are compared to the rest of the city."

It was a view of the city many had never seen before.

nhep.com

tre scalini

executive chef | Joseph Maiorano

In the heart of New Haven's Italian neighborhood, a fine dining restaurant such as Tre Scalini offers a calm, comfortable alternative to the tumult of Wooster Street's famous pizzerias.

Joseph Maiorano opened Tre Scalini in 1995 and in doing so came home to his birthplace. Joe was born in the building, and his father left retirement to run a cheese shop in one of the storefronts. After Joe bought the building in the 1970s, a succession of Italian eateries occupied the space until he decided to try his hand at running a restaurant.

The menu, which changes every six months, offers regional Italian dishes with an emphasis on Neapolitan specialties. Joe says that his most popular dishes aren't traditionally Italian: beef filet with lobster meat in a Gorgonzola cream sauce and Pappardelle al Telefono, broad egg noodles and lobster meat in a light pink sauce. The tastefully decorated dining room with tall windows overlooking the street, pale gold walls, tin ceiling, and artwork feel like a cozy ristorante in the Tuscan countryside.

100 Wooster St. | 203.777.3373
trescalinirestaurant.com

Scrod Marechiaro

Fresh scrod with littleneck clams in a light pomodoro sauce are served over angel hair pasta.

¼ cup extra-virgin olive oil

4 cloves garlic, minced

3 cups Italian tomato sauce

5 basil leaves, chopped

1 teaspoon salt, plus more for pasta water

2 pinches freshly ground black pepper

1 box angel hair pasta

24 littleneck clams

4 8-ounce scrod fillets

1. Put a pot of water on high heat to boil for the pasta. Combine olive oil and garlic in a sauté pan over medium-high heat; sauté until garlic is golden brown. Add tomato sauce, basil, salt, and pepper. Cook for 1 to 2 minutes.

2. Add salt to the boiling water, then the pasta. Cook pasta until al dente, according to cooking instructions on package.

3. Add the clams and scrod to the tomato mixture and cover sauté pan. Cook until clams open, about 8 minutes.

4. Drain pasta, put it in a large bowl, and pour the sauce, clams, and scrod over the pasta.

union league cafe

executive chef | Jean Pierre Vuillermet

The walk under the ornate Sherman's Arch and into the wide brick alleyway is the first step to an experience equal to dining at a Parisian brasserie. Before the landmark Sherman building became the domain of chef-owner Jean Pierre Vuillermet, the exquisite Beaux Arts structure was a private home and the Union League Club. Architectural touches such as high ceilings, mahogany molding and mantles, and marble pillars give the dining room a distinctive character.

A fixture in New Haven since 1993, the cafe is a shining example of French service and cuisine in a city that has the most varied ethnic restaurant scene in Connecticut. Chef Jean Pierre builds on the classic dishes of his homeland, adding contemporary touches to keep his knowledgeable following surprised and delighted. "It's amazing the change in how much people know about food," he says, citing travel and television programs as factors.

For the adventurous, the chef changes the menu every month or two, but there are certain dishes that the faithful expect to see: "The duck confit and the spinach salad, we cannot take off the menu. It's kind of a comfort feeling. They are dishes that customers can rely on."

1032 Chapel St. | 203.562.4299
unionleaguecafe.com

Cod Chowder

I love this dish, especially when corn is in season. This chowder has a New England feel and is very versatile. It can serve as a soup, an appetizer, or a one-dish meal. When we make it at the restaurant, I can't stop sampling it! —JEAN PIERRE

1 tablespoon butter or olive oil

1 tablespoon diced chorizo sausage

½ red onion, chopped

1 scallion, chopped

½ cup fresh corn kernels

1 leek, washed and minced

1 clove garlic

4 threads saffron

¼ teaspoon fresh thyme leaves

1 bay leaf

8 fingerling potatoes, cut into ⅓-inch dice

1 cup clam juice

2 cups heavy cream

Salt and freshly ground black pepper

16 littleneck clams, steamed open and shucked

1 tablespoon chopped fresh flat-leaf parsley

1 pound cod fillet, cut into 4 pieces

Olive oil

1. Heat the butter or olive oil in a large frying pan over medium-high heat. Add the chorizo, red onion, scallion, corn, and leek and sauté until onion softens, stirring often.

2. Add the garlic, saffron, thyme, and bay leaf, and sauté for 2 more minutes.

3. Add the diced potatoes, clam juice, and heavy cream, and cook until the potatoes are tender but still firm. Add salt and pepper to taste. Add the steamed clams and parsley, then set aside, keeping warm.

4. Roast the cod in olive oil by broiling in the oven until desired doneness. Place roasted cod on top of hot chowder.

5. Drizzle each serving with olive oil.

Almond Cake

This is an upgraded pound cake for the almond lover. When I serve this cake at home, it is usually an accompaniment to roasted peaches or a fresh berry compote. My friends and family usually ask for a second serving of cake, forgetting the fruits altogether. —JEAN PIERRE

1. Preheat the oven to 350°F. Butter an 8-inch cake pan. Sift the flour and cornstarch together; set aside.

2. In a medium saucepan over medium-high heat, melt the butter until it starts to lightly brown. Remove from heat and add liquors. Stir in the flour mixture; set aside.

3. Place the marzipan in the bowl of a stand mixer fitted with the paddle attachment. Mix the marzipan, to soften. Add the eggs one at a time, mixing well after each addition.

4. Mix one-third of the marzipan-egg mixture into the flour-butter mixture. Incorporate the remaining marzipan-egg mixture with a spatula.

5. Sprinkle the sliced almonds in the prepared pan, covering the bottom and sides of the pan. Pour the batter into the pan.

6. Place pan in oven and bake for 30 minutes or until a knife inserted in the center comes out clean.

7. Invert the cake onto a serving platter and allow to cool. Sprinkle with confectioners' sugar.

3 cups cake flour

2 tablespoons cornstarch

6 tablespoons butter

1 teaspoon rum

1 teaspoon Grand Marnier

10 ounces marzipan

4 large eggs

¼ cup sliced almonds

Confectioners' sugar

zinc &
kitchen zinc

executive chef | Denise Appel

During construction of Zinc in 1999, co-owners Donna Curran and Denise Appel looked at the Z-shaped door handles, a holdover from the Zoon gallery that had previously occupied the space, and tagged them for removal. As the work progressed, their impression of the letters on the main entrance changed. They scrapped their list of twenty-five possible names and zeroed in on the end of the alphabet.

Zinc, chosen for the casual, neighborhood zinc bars of France, saved the handles and set the "global, worldly" tone that Donna and Denise envisioned for their guests. The focal point of the sleek, modern decor is an eight-foot zinc-covered table. Wooden tables and metal accents exude the same minimalist feel in Zinc's sister restaurant, Kitchen Zinc, a pizza, salad, and charcuterie emporium tucked into an alley next to the original eatery.

In both restaurants, locally grown and artisanal ingredients are staples. Chef Denise borrows techniques and flavors from the world's cuisines to enliven Zinc's New American seasonal menus and the artisan pies at Kitchen Zinc. A prix fixe market menu during the growing season and free weekly wine tastings give the faithful more reasons to open those Z doors.

Zinc
964 Chapel St. | 203.624.0507
zincfood.com

Kitchen Zinc
203.772.3002
kitchenzinc.com

Market Vegetable Rice-Paper Rolls with Yuzu Sauce

Locally grown and seasonally fresh, just as the name implies, almost every fresh ingredient here can be found at your local farmers' market.

For the yuzu dipping sauce:

1 teaspoon chopped garlic

¼ cup sugar

2 tablespoons rice vinegar

2 tablespoons soy sauce

Pinch of freshly ground black pepper

2 tablespoons yuzu sauce*

For the rice-paper rolls:

1 medium-size cucumber, sliced thin

10 fresh breakfast radishes, sliced thin

¼ cup rice vinegar

2 tablespoons sugar

Pinch of crushed red pepper flakes

2 tablespoons sriracha sauce*

1 package rice paper*

4 large red-leaf lettuce leaves

1 bunch fresh Thai basil

Rice paper, sriracha sauce, and yuzu sauce can be found in Asian markets.

1. To prepare the yuzu dipping sauce, mix all ingredients together.

2. To prepare the rice-paper rolls, mix sliced cucumber and radish together, add rice vinegar, sugar, crushed red pepper, and sriracha and stir to blend. Let sit for 10 minutes.

3. Place 2 rice-paper sheets in a bowl of warm water and let paper become soft, 1 minute. Remove from water and place on a clean surface.

4. Divide red-leaf lettuce, cucumber and radish (no liquid), and Thai basil between 2 rice-paper leaves. Fold the left and right sides of one of the rice papers over the filling, like you were going to roll a cigar. Then fold the bottom of the rice paper over the filling and begin to roll upward, forming the cigar, trying to keep it tight. Let the roll rest for a minute, so it absorbs all of the water. Repeat with the remaining rice-paper roll.

5. Serve with the yuzu dipping sauce.

Smoked Salmon Tostadas with Red Pepper Salsa

This dish serves well as an appetizer, a first course, or small plate (tapas). Beautiful *and* tasty, the presentation and flavors are sure to please.

For the salmon:

½ pound good-quality smoked salmon

¼ cup diced red onion

Pinch of freshly ground black pepper

2 tablespoons chopped chives

For the red pepper salsa:

2 fresh red bell peppers*

2 tablespoons olive oil, plus more for peppers

¼ cup finely chopped red onion

Dash of white balsamic vinegar

Pinch of freshly ground black pepper

2 tablespoons chopped chives

For the tostadas:

5 cups canola oil

1 package corn tortillas

Salt

Fresh cilantro, chopped, for garnish

You can also use good-quality canned roasted red peppers instead. Pat the peppers dry to remove some of their canning juice.

1. To prepare the salmon, cut it into short, thin strips. Place salmon strips, red onion, black pepper, and chives in a bowl. Mix to combine and set aside.

2. To prepare the salsa, rub the bell peppers with olive oil. Using tongs, a long-handled fork, or a skewer, hold peppers over a gas flame and char the peppers, turning often. When evenly charred, place in a plastic bag for about 3 minutes, until skin releases. Remove skin.

3. Roughly chop the roasted peppers and place in a bowl. Then add the onion, balsamic vinegar, 2 tablespoons olive oil, black pepper, and chives.

4. To prepare the tostadas, heat the canola oil in a large frying pan on medium-high for about 10 minutes. Do not let oil get hot enough to smoke.

5. Cut the tortillas into pieces of desired size. Place a few pieces at a time into the heated oil. Fry until golden. With tongs, remove from the oil and place on paper towel or an absorbent paper plate. Lightly salt the tostadas.

6. Place the tostadas on a plate and add a small mound of salmon mixture to each piece. Top each with a spoonful of the red pepper salsa, and garnish with a pinch of chopped cilantro.

index

Contributing writers and photographers:

Amy Etra is a Connecticut based photographer who has been shooting for over 30 years. This project, photographed over the past 2 years, reflects the artistry and skill she has mastered over her long and varied career. To see more of Amy's work, please go to amyetra.com

Jan Ellen Spiegel is a longtime print, television, and radio journalist and award-winning food editor and writer who lives (cooks and eats) in the New Haven area. Her work has been published in the *New York Times,* the *Hartford Courant, Saveur, Connecticut Magazine* and many other publications and broadcast outlets. She is looking forward to a day that she won't have to wait in line to get into one of New Haven's legendary pizza places.

Todd Lyon is a freelance writer who has been covering the restaurant scene in New Haven County for 20 years. She is the author/co-author of 17 books, mostly about pleasurable subjects like parties, fashion, kissing and food. Her column, "Deep Dish," appears in the *New Haven Register.*

Valerie Bannister is a freelance writer and photographer. She lives in Chester, Connecticut with her two daughters, Maggie and Britta.

Sharon Vine is a New Haven native, photographer and stylist. She currently works between Connecticut and New York City while living with her fiance Mike in Black Rock, Connecticut.